Reviving Christian Humanism

"Erudite and accessible, Browning's scholarship once again cuts a clear path through a dense forest of ideas now growing at the interface of religion and morality. His nuanced distinctions between ethics and morality, religion and spirituality, and foundationalist and hermeneutic epistemological approaches are among the most helpful to be found in the literature. He offers original and constructive direction for continued research through his critical but congenial engagement with recent thinking in positive and moral psychology. I know of no higher praise than to say I look forward to sharing his insights with my students as soon as possible."
Michael Leffel, Professor of Psychology
Point Loma Nazarene University

"No one is more equipped than Don Browning to discuss the relationship between theology, psychology, and spirituality. Bringing a very seasoned, interdisciplinary background to this discussion, Browning demonstrates how a hermeneutical perspective can employ science as a very important 'submoment' within a larger interpretive framework and conversation. Browning brings together insights from a long and distinguished career as he points the way toward a religious humanism for the twenty-first century."
Terry D. Cooper, Professor of Psychology
St. Louis Community College

"Don Browning once again draws on his encyclopedic knowledge of theology, psychology, cognitive and social neurosciences, and the law to illustrate the deep ways in which science and religion require each other. From the perspective of a decades-long career, he revisits his earlier observations of psychotherapy, marriage, and religious institutions and demonstrates the urgent need for a public philosophy for science and the mental health disciplines as well as for theology. The book is a must-read for clinicians, theologians, and all who are interested in the larger science and religion conversation."
David Hogue, Professor of Pastoral Theology and Counseling
Garrett-Evangelical Theological Seminary

THEOLOGY AND THE SCIENCES
Kevin J. Sharpe, Founding Editor

BOARD OF ADVISORS

TITLES IN THE SERIES

Nature, Reality, and the Sacred
Langdon Gilkey

The Human Factor
Philip Hefner

On the Moral Nature of the Universe
Nancey Murphy and George F. R. Ellis

Theology for a Scientific Age
Arthur Peacocke

The Faith of a Physicist
John Polkinghorne

The Travail of Nature
H. Paul Santmire

God, Creation,
and Contemporary Physics
Mark William Worthing

Unprecedented Choices
Audrey R. Chapman

Whatever Happened to the Soul?
Warren S. Brown, Nancey Murphy,
and H. Newton Malony, editors

The Mystical Mind
Eugene d'Aquili and Andrew B. Newberg

Nature Reborn
H. Paul Santmire

Wrestling with the Divine
Christopher C. Knight

The Garden of God
Alejandro Garcia-Rivera

Doing without Adam and Eve
Patricia A. Williams

Nature, Human Nature, and God
Ian G. Barbour

In Our Image
Noreen L. Herzfeld

Minding God
Gregory R. Peterson

Light from the East
Alexei V. Nesteruk

Participating in God
Samuel M. Powell

Adam, Eve, and the Genome
Susan Brooks Thistlethwaite, editor

Bridging Science and Religion
Ted Peters and Gaymon Bennett, editors

Minding the Soul
James B. Ashbrook

The Music of Creation
Arthur Peacocke and Ann Pederson

Creation and Double Chaos
Sjoerd L. Bonting

The Living Spirit of the Crone
Sally Palmer Thomason

All That Is
Arthur Peacocke

Reviving Christian Humanism
Don S. Browning

Reviving Christian Humanism

The New Conversation on Spirituality, Theology, and Psychology

Don S. Browning

FORTRESS PRESS
MINNEAPOLIS

REVIVING CHRISTIAN HUMANISM
The New Conversation on Spirituality, Theology, and Psychology

Cover image: "Three People around the Sun" by Nicholas Wilton

Library of Congress Cataloging-in-Publication Data
Browning, Don S.
  Reviving Christian humanism : the new conversation on spirituality, theology, and psychology / Don S. Browning.
      p. cm.
  Book evolved from six lectures given by the author at Boston University.
  Includes bibliographical references.
  ISBN 978-0-8006-9626-9 (alk. paper)
  1. Psychology and religion. 2. Humanism. 3. Christianity-Philosophy. 4. Science and religion. I. Title.
  BF51.B77 2010
  261.5'15—dc22
                              2009029479

15   14   13   12   11   10   1 2 3 4 5 6 7 8 9 10

Contents

Preface

This book evolved from six lectures I gave at Boston University in October and November, 2008. I used them to advance a thesis that has been appearing more frequently in my recent writing: that the emerging dialogue between science and religion can help revive both religious and Christian humanism. By *Christian humanism*, I have in mind various historic expressions of Christianity that were concerned with the spiritual goods of salvation and justification as well as the finite and inner-worldly goods of health, education, and sufficient wealth to sustain a decent life in this world. Furthermore, when Christian humanism is vital, it generally is in conversation with science and philosophy in an effort to further clarify the finite goods of human life. Christian humanism gains insights from science and philosophy about the rhythms of nature that Christian theology must necessarily assume when developing its ethics and social theory.

My central argument is that Christian humanism in particular, and religious humanism in general, can best be revived if the conversation between science and religion proceeds within what I call a "critical hermeneutic philosophy." I try to explain and illustrate what this point of view can contribute to both the science-religion discussion and the strengthening of religious and Christian humanism.

I distinguish Christian from religious humanism. Christian humanism takes as its point of departure the multifaceted strands of the Christian tradition. It tries to relate to science out of the depths of this complex tradition—a tradition that has dominated in the West, shaped many of its institutions and much of its law, and placed a stamp on most of its academic disciplines. Because of the influence of Christianity on Western culture, it deserves to be much better understood than it currently is in much academic and cultural discourse. We should study this Christian heritage because it is in our bones—even the bones of the unbeliever—in ways we often do not understand. It comes down to this: we cannot understand ourselves unless we understand what historical forces have shaped us, and Christianity is certainly one of those central influences.

By *religious humanism*, I mean to suggest that many of the other great religious traditions of the world—for example, Confucianism, Hinduism, Buddhism, Judaism, and Islam—also have their humanistic dimensions. They have, at times, had their dialogues with the science and philosophy available in their respective cultures. They too can cultivate, strengthen, and revive their historical moments of religious humanism. But even here, I recommend working within the resources of specific traditions to revive the various religious humanisms. I do not advocate trying to develop some general religious humanism that transcends specific traditions and offers some homogenized and nonhistorical spirituality that is unrecognizable from the perspective of any specific religious faith. I say, instead, that in conversation with the sciences—particularly the psychological and social sciences—we should revive the humanistic dimensions of our various grand religious traditions and then enter into an interfaith dialogue with a sharper grasp of our various world religious humanisms.

My colleague and lunch partner, William Schweiker, works more with the category of theological humanism in contrast to religious or Christian humanism, although he appreciates these labels as well. By *theological humanism*, he means a critical perspective on Christian theology that includes but goes beyond confession and thereby enters into a reflective dialogue with both nontheological disciplines and other faiths.[1] He believes that elements of this agenda can be found in other religions as well as Christianity and that this critical reflective attitude should be encouraged in both interfaith dialogue and the emerging field of comparative religious ethics. I agree. When I use the term *religious humanism*, I mean to include the possibility of this critical reflective stance as central to the strategy of strengthening and revival that I am proposing.

Summaries of books are never fun to read. They tend to be too condensed and abstract. Because the meat is not in the advanced review of the argument, the bones themselves seem all the more dry. Nonetheless, the arguments of this small book are complex. The range of references covers several disciplines. It is an interdisciplinary study. Although the relation of science to religion is the overall topic, I make use of perspectives in the philosophy of religion, the philosophy of science, theology, moral philosophy, psychology, psychotherapy, neuroscience, evolutionary psychology, sociology, economics, and law. So, a sketch of the content and argument might prove helpful, even if tedious to read the first time through. Furthermore, readers might profit from an occasional glance back to this summary as they go through the text—lending a little extra help to keep the argument straight.

The first chapter, "Science, Religion, and a Revived Religious Humanism," announces the central concern and basic methodology of this study. It advances the thesis, already announced above, that a possible consequence of the dialogue between science and religion is a revived religious humanism—a firmer grasp of the historical and phenomenological meanings of the great world religions correlated with the more accurate explanations of the rhythms of nature that natural science can provide. Although there are hints of interaction between Greek science and philosophy with the teachings of early Christianity, the first great expressions of religious humanism in the West emerged when Jewish, Christian, and Islamic scholars sat in the same libraries in Spain and Sicily, studying and translating the lost manuscripts of Aristotle in the ninth and tenth centuries to understand his ethics, epistemology, and psychobiology. This study established strands of Jewish, Christian, and Islamic humanism that are important models even for the needs of today.

Other religious traditions have their moments of religious humanism as well. Chapter 1 also argues that, in our day, the science-religion dialogue—exemplified by interaction among psychology, spirituality, and psychotherapy—will best support such a revival if guided by the philosophical resources of critical hermeneutics (sometimes called hermeneutical realism) supplemented by William James's brand of phenomenology and pragmatism. In this chapter, I develop primarily the contributions of Paul Ricoeur to hermeneutic realism and his unique ability to find a place for the natural sciences within hermeneutic phenomenology in his formula of understanding-explanation-understanding—his useful epistemological summary for relating the humanities to science. James's contribution is developed in later chapters.

In chapter 2, "Broadening Psychology, Refining Theology," I argue that the payoff of this strategy will be to both broaden the subject matter of psychology and refine assumptions about nature in religious traditions. Since I am a Christian practical theologian, I exemplify these claims chiefly with Christian materials and occasional references to folk and other axial religions. I hope that readers who are not Christians will follow me into this discussion, not because I hope to convert them but because I want to illustrate how science can help refine religious traditions rather than to attack or dismantle them.

In chapter 2, I offer two case studies of how Christian theology can be refined and how psychology can be broadened. I first do this by looking at the implications for the so-called Christian doctrine of the atonement as to how empathy works change in psychotherapy and how "radical empathy" works change in the healing rites of folk religions. Here I have in mind the debate in Christian theologies of the atonement among Christus victor models, penal substitutionary models, and moral influence models of the efficacy of Christ's death. Advances in the social neurosciences on radical empathy and simulation theory lead me to see the strengths of Christ's identification with the suffering of humankind in the Christus victor model.

The second illustration brings natural-science work on love and loneliness to the debate among the *eros*, *caritas*, and *agape* views of the nature of Christian love. I argue that new understandings of the role of the affections in attachment theory and evolutionary psychology tilt the argument toward the caritas model. Science will do better if it works hard to understand (in the sense of *verstehen)* the complexity of religious traditions. This will help science comprehend that what it offers as critiques of religions are often actually refinements of traditions that have had ongoing conversations about competing interpretations. This attitude will help science—including the psychological sciences—develop new hypotheses about how cultures and religions shape experience. The chapter concludes by clarifying my own Christology as it has developed over the years and by defending the need to locate spirituality within the category of religion.

In chapter 3, "Change and Critique in Psychology, Therapy, and Spirituality," I contend that changing people in psychology, therapy, and spirituality is not enough. We should be able to critique these claims about change. Not all change is for the good in the long run, even if we are tempted to welcome a brief moment of relief or reorientation. In my earlier work, I joined with Robert Bellah, Christopher Lasch, and, later, Frank Richardson in being somewhat critical of the individualism promoted by much of psychotherapy. Some people make the same charge against our culture's new fascination with the category of spirituality. I confess in this chapter that I may have overstated the implicit individualism of the modern therapies. But I also defend my earlier interest in assessing the views of health and human fulfillment in the modern psychologies and psychotherapies.

Now, however, I bring into play the moral anthropology of Paul Ricoeur to help with this task. I set forth his distinction between ethics (striving to attain the goods of life) and morality (concern to resolve conflicts among goods). I compare his view with the distinctions between nonmoral and moral goods in moral philosopher William Frankena and between premoral and moral goods in the Catholic moral theologian Louis Janssens. I also show how Ricoeur locates this distinction between ethics and morality with reference to his theory of practice, narrative, the deontological critique, and wisdom in the concrete situation. I then locate the contributions and limitations of views about the goals of change in some personality and therapeutic theories, evolutionary psychology, Jonathan Haidt's moral intuitionism, neuroscientist Donald Pfaff's explanation of the Golden Rule, and Lawrence Kohlberg's Kantian-oriented moral psychology. I show that many of the modern psychologies have much to offer to our attempts to define what Ricoeur calls ethics or Janssens calls the premoral good, but they have less to contribute to defining morality in its fuller sense. This has implications for assessing the goals of change proffered by these disciplines and practices.

In chapter 4, "Religion, Science, and the New Spirituality," I turn to the dialogue among these three elements. I carry this inquiry into a more detailed look at spirituality—more specifically, into what I take to be the way the science-religion dialogue is now shaping spirituality. I claim that, along with other modern trends, science is influencing spirituality to give more attention to relationships (attachments and family), work or vocation, and practical reason. Modern medicine is interested in the health values of spirituality. Modern psychology of religion is concerned with how spirituality influences relationships, marriage, sexuality, work, health, wealth, and citizenship. I review examples of the positive psychology movement that illustrate its tendency to evaluate spiritualities from these frameworks and sometimes make uninformed judgments about what some claim to be Buddhism's rejection of human relationships and Christianity's abstract and overly idealistic view of love. This may be another illustration of science failing to precede explanation (and its implicit critiques) with adequate understanding (*verstehen*) of the ongoing debates over interpretation within particular religious traditions.

I then discuss the double entendres of the language of finite goods and transcendent realities that float through much contemporary therapeutic and spiritual language. I contend that natural scientists should both notice this double language and grasp why humans tend to talk at two levels of meaning (mundane and transcendent) at the same time, especially about healing. Rather than prematurely rejecting this language as an aberration, science should try instead to understand what these levels of meaning do for each other. I end with a brief review of how Ignatius Loyola informed the values of family (relationships), work (career and vocation), and practical reason with his view of the moral implications of Christian ethics and narrative. Ignatius may give us a clue as to what the more transcendent aspects of some spiritualities can contribute to the new interest in family, work, and practical reason in recent developments in spirituality.

In chapter 5, "Mental Health and Spirituality: Their Institutional Embodiments," I turn to neglected institutional considerations of the science-religion dialogue. I hold that it is essential to the revival of a viable religious humanism to consider the institutional embodiments of religious experience and sensibility—a theme that began to emerge in chapter 2. In addition, I argue that the institutional embodiments of religious experience need orchestration with other institutions, including the mental health institutions. I give special attention to the mental health institution of psychiatry in this chapter. Philosopher Kwame Appiah, in his response to the moral intuitionism of Joshua Green and Jonathan Haidt, points out that if our moral thinking is shaped first by primitive intuitions—such as in-group/out-group, respect for hierarchy, and purity and disgust—with only moderate influence from our higher deliberative capacities, this may argue only for the importance of the ongoing and slow moral reflective processes of institutions in modern societies.

This insight into the importance of institutions leads me to call for a public philosophy for psychiatry in its relation to the other institutions of society, including religious institutions. I quote evidence that psychiatry has relinquished its earlier concern, evident between 1940 and 1970, with mental health and psychotherapy and in recent decades has narrowed its interests to mental states that can be addressed with psychopharmacology. I summarize social science evidence indicating that psychiatry has inadequately studied religion and its contributions to human well-being. There is further evidence that psychiatry and American religious institutions are somewhat alienated from each other and that this distrust partially explains the rise among religious bodies of alternative mental health systems, sometimes of an explicitly religious kind. I examine how Ricoeur's dialectic between understanding-explanation-understanding supplemented by William James's wedding of his brand of phenomenology with the consequentialism of his pragmatism can together be resources for a public philosophy of psychiatry in relation to religious institutions. Such an orchestration of mental health institutions and religious institutions may be essential for reviving religious and, more specifically, Christian humanism.

Finally, in chapter 6, "Institutional Ethics and Families: Therapy, Law, and Religion," I carry further the institutional aspects of the dialogue between science and religion as exemplified by the contemporary interaction among psychology, psychotherapy, and spirituality. In the course of these lectures, the institutional aspects of the science-religion dialogue have become increasingly salient. I raise this issue again by discussing the unavoidable encounters among marriage and family therapy, law, and various religious traditions.

I summarize in that final chapter published empirical evidence showing that several subdisciplines of marriage and family therapy, while not completely agreeing about ethical issues they face in their work, have amazing areas of consensus. In fact, there may be implicit in their shared moral sensibilities the nucleus of a public philosophy for this specialty of the mental health field. The various family and marriage counselors surveyed—psychiatrists, psychologists, social workers, pastoral counselors, marriage and family therapists—are surprisingly traditional in their views of marriage, family, and what is good for children. They are not individualistic, or at least not as much so, as is often thought. Rather, they hold what our survey report called an ethic of *relationality*. This flies in the face of widespread charges about the implicit individualistic ethic of the modern therapies; this complaint does not seem to apply to marriage and family therapists.

But an ethic of relationality does not solve everything and can itself have surprising, and possibly negative, implications if taken in certain directions. I summarize my recent work in family-law theory and show how the therapeutic emphasis on family relationality and process is used by law, along with other justifications, to argue for either the delegalization of marriage or the functional equivalence of cohabitation and legal marriage. This, in many ways, puts the results of our national survey of the ethics of family and marriage counselors at odds with the dominant direction of U.S. family-law theory today. I conclude with an appreciative review of the legal theories of Margaret Brinig, who synthesizes a phenomenology of Western religious covenant theory, evolutionary psychology, and the new institutional economics to build a fresh justification for maintaining the "signaling" and "channeling" functions of legal marriage. This is supported by her highly respected empirical research with University of Virginia sociologist Steven Nock on the importance of legal institutions in guiding personal and public behavior. I contend that marriage and family therapists, in their own efforts to orchestrate their work with other institutions, need to confront the tensions on the borderline between law, psychology, and religion. Such a dialogue is also important for a revived religious humanism.

I conclude with a summary of the argument and a forecast for the future of the science-religion dialogue. I contend that the dialogue among psychology, psychotherapy, and spirituality is crucial to combat both the new fundamentalists of our day and the new atheists who advance allegedly scientific justifications for their positions. A third alternative to these two contending cultural movements is a revived religious humanism in general and a revived Christian humanism in particular. I end by saying more about the importance of spirituality to be embodied within ongoing religious institutions and traditions and not just a free-standing, individualistic source of comfort and well-being.

Acknowledgments

This book was originally presented as the Templeton Lectures at Boston University in autumn 2008. These lectures were commissioned by the interdisciplinary faculty research group on science and religion sponsored by the Danielson Institute—a clinical psychotherapeutic service, training, and research facility at Boston University. They were supported by a generous gift from the Templeton Foundation.

The assigned title of the lectures was "Psychotherapy, Psychology, and Spirituality." The larger framework for the lectures was the emerging and more general dialogue between science and religion. These lectures are about the significance of this dialogue, and I use the growing conversation among psychotherapy, psychology, and spirituality as a way of illustrating my point of view. When discussing psychology, I also address some of the important new insights and challenges coming from the subdisciplines of moral psychology, social neuroscience, cognitive science, and evolutionary psychology.

I want to express my gratitude to Professor Robert Neville, director of the Danielson Institute, for his very generous hospitality and encouragement. I also want to thank two of his associates, Nat Barrett and Sarah Clough, for their warmth and the help they provided with logistics. I also want to thank members of the science and religion group who, along with the general public, attended these lectures and discussed our mutual interests.

Giving these lectures allowed me to look back over my long career of thinking and writing about the relation of psychology and psychotherapy to religion and spirituality and to review some of my older perspectives in light of new advances in these disciplines. I am deeply grateful to the Templeton Foundation and the Danielson Institute for inviting me to give these lectures and then make them available in this book.

1

Science, Religion, and a Revived Religious Humanism

For over 150 years there has been a vital, and often contentious, dialogue between science and religion. In recent years, new energy and fresh public interest have been injected into this conversation. This largely has come about due to the new insights into religion and ethics achieved by collaboration between evolutionary psychology and cognitive and social neuroscience.

What are the likely social consequences of this new interest in the relation of science and religion? There are at least three possible answers. One might be the new atheism exemplified by the writings of Richard Dawkins, Daniel Dennett, Sam Harris, and Christopher Hitchens.[1] In this approach, the alleged defective thinking of the world religions is exposed, and a worldview and way of life based strictly on science are offered as replacement. A second option might be the return of a hegemonic dominance of religion over science. A third might be the emergence of a revitalized religious humanism of the kind that has happened on several occasions in the past in most of the great world religions. This last option is the one I will advocate.

What would this religious humanism be like? The major world religions would remain visible and viable as religious movements. But the contributions of science would help these religions refine their interests in improving the health, education, wealth, and overall well-being of their adherents and the general population. In addition, the sciences would help them refine their grasp of the empirical world, about which they, like humans in general, are constantly making judgments, predictions, and characterizations. In my vision, the attitude of scientists toward religion would be first of all phenomenological; they would first attempt to describe and understand (in the sense of *verstehen*) religious beliefs, ethics, and rituals in their full historical context. But their interest in explaining some of the conditions that give rise to religious phenomena would not be inhibited by either religion or the wider society. Yet the wiser scientists would understand the limits of explanation, would hesitate to skip lightly over the initial phenomenological moment, and would be reluctant to plunge headlong into speculations about the ultimate truth or falsity of religious ideas and practices in the way exhibited by the new scientific atheism.

On the other hand, the religions themselves can contribute to the sciences by offering hypotheses about how social and religious ideas, behaviors, and rituals can shape experience, even neural processes, often for the good but sometimes not. The religions can offer a more generous epistemology and ontology than science is inclined to find useful for the tight explanatory interests of the laboratory or scientific survey. This too might generate new hypotheses for scientific investigation. These would be some of the ground rules for how a dialogue between science and religion might stimulate a revived religious humanism.

Religious Humanisms of the Past

To speak of a revival of religious humanism acknowledges that there have been many expressions of religious humanism in the past. I will limit myself to speaking primarily about Judaism, Christianity, and Islam. The synthesis between Greek philosophical psychology and Christianity can be found in the use of Stoic theories of desire by the apostle Paul,[2] the presence of Aristotle's family ethic in the household codes of Ephesians and 1 Colossians,[3] and the Gospel of John's identification of Jesus with the Platonic and Stoic idea of the preexistent "Word."[4] A more intentional religious humanism can be found in Augustine's use of the neoplatonic Plotinus, especially in the philosophical psychology of remembrance in his *Confessions* (397 A.D.).[5]

But the most dramatic example of a religious humanism that spread simultaneously into Judaism, Christianity, and Islam can be found when the lost texts of Aristotle were discovered, translated, and appropriated by scholars from these three religions who worked at the same tables in Islamic libraries in Spain and Sicily during the ninth and tenth centuries. Richard Rubinstein, in his timely book titled *Aristotle's Children* (2003), tells the story well.[6] This study gave rise to forms of Aristotelian religious humanism in the works of Thomas Aquinas in Christianity, Maimonides in Judaism, and Averroës in Islam. On the American scene, one sees another form of Christian humanism in the synthesis of philosophical pragmatism, with all its influence from Darwin, and various expressions of liberal Christianity and the social gospel movement.[7]

Religious humanisms have not always flourished and are subject to attacks from both fundamentalists and scientific secularists. They need constant updating and vigorous intellectual development. But at their best, they make it possible for societies to maintain strong religious communities as well as integrating symbolic umbrellas that protect the productive interaction of the scientific and philosophical disciplines with the wider cultural and religious life.

Epistemological Frameworks for a Revived Religious Humanism

But on what epistemological and ontological grounds could such a dialogue between science and religion proceed today, especially if they were supportive of a revived religious humanism? In this book, I will address this question as a Christian theologian. Furthermore, most of my illustrations will come from the Christian tradition. Although I am interested in the possibility of a more widespread revival of religious humanism in Judaism, Islam, and the other great world religions, my illustrations and arguments will feature the tradition I know best. This will be useful for another reason. Of all the great world religions, for a variety of internal and external historical reasons, Christianity has doubtless had the most vigorous encounter to date with the challenges and stimulations of the rise of science in the modern world.

In my effort to demonstrate how the dialogue between science and religion can be productive, I will go two directions at once with varying degrees of evenness. To say it crassly, like the philosophical pragmatist that I am, I will try to show the payoff for both Christianity on the one hand and selected psychological disciplines on the other. I will attempt to show what Christianity can learn from some aspects of science that will refine, and in this sense improve, its grasp of its own religious beliefs, ethics, worship, healing, and spiritual practices. But I will also suggest ways in which these scientific disciplines can profit. By "profit," however, I do not mean just getting more money in their research accounts, although that may happen as well. As I have already indicated, the modern psychologies, even in their properly naturalistic forms, can gain new hypotheses about how experience, including religious experience, shapes feelings, motivations, neural processes, and behaviors. With the advent of positive psychology in the work of Martin Seligman, Jonathan Haidt, Joshua Greene, and many others, an entire range of new research topics has emerged around love, forgiveness, wisdom, virtue, and spiritual transformation that was almost entirely absent from the psychological disciplines as recently as a decade ago.

We live in a period of wider and more fruitful epistemologies that open new possibilities of research between science and religion, even between psychology and Christian theology, that need not threaten either and could indeed strengthen them both. I have been retired from the Divinity School of the University of Chicago for over six years. Since the time of my official departure, several new collaborative research projects involving the natural sciences and the humanities—including theology and religious studies—have emerged around this university, which historically has been dedicated to graduate education and research. Today there are collaborative projects involving the natural sciences and the humanities that are proceeding on such diverse topics as spirituality and health, a science of virtue, wisdom, decision making, and anthropomorphism. They involve social neuroscientists, philosophers, political theorists, medical doctors, philosophers, social psychologists, sociologists, and theologians. Such collaboration at this university between science and the humanities would have been unthinkable during the peak of my active teaching years. It is interesting to note that the stimulators of much of this collaboration come from the burgeoning field of social neuroscience and such innovative and ecumenical scholars as John Cacioppo and Howard Nusbaum. Their knowledge of the neural plasticity of the human brain leads them to be as interested in how the external influences of social, cultural, and religious experience shape the physical base of our mental processes as they are in how these brain processes project themselves into our thoughts and behaviors.

I recall a prediction made to me by a distinguished New York University psychologist in the early 1990s. He believed that the rise of the neurosciences would relegate most of traditional psychology to the humanities and that departments of psychology would become branches of biology and medicine. I can remember leaving his office in a slight fog of depression over hearing this possibility. In many places, however, just the reverse has happened. A new conversation between psychology as a natural science and the humanities has risen that may have immense fruitfulness for both fields of study.

But what epistemological and ontological frameworks should guide such a conversation and possible collaboration? I will propose in these lectures the resources of what the late French philosopher Paul Ricoeur would call either *critical hermeneutics* or *hermeneutic phenomenology*. I can imagine that the very sound of these technical terms sends icy chills down the spines of some readers. I will try to explain them the best I can as I develop my arguments.

I can say this much now. There have been in recent years important and powerful proposals about the significance of phenomenology for the psychological disciplines, especially the clinical disciplines. These have been advanced by Frank Richardson, Blaine Fowers, and Charles Guignon in *Re-envisioning Psychology* (1999) and by Philip Cushman in *Constructing the Self, Constructing America: A Cultural History of Psychotherapy* (1995).[8] But, from my perspective, these proposals move too far in the direction of making psychology a thoroughly interpretive discipline, nearly losing the element of objectivity, or what I will call, following Ricoeur, the moments of distanciation and explanation that psychology as a science also must always include. But I say these things now only to chart the course I will travel. I will say more about these cryptic remarks in a moment.

I start first, however, with the term *hermeneutic phenomenology*. Hermeneutic phenomenology is an offshoot of the European hermeneutical and phenomenological movements. The hermeneutic side ran through the work of German theologian Friedrich Schleiermacher, the historian Wilhelm Dilthey, and the philosophers Martin Heidegger, Hans-Georg Gadamer, and Paul Ricoeur. This movement was concerned with questions about the appropriate interpretation of texts. It held that the quests for meaning by the human spirit were objectified in the great texts of the past, and that to retain this fund of meaning and insight, these texts required interpretation and internalization.[9] The hermeneutic movement arose from the disciplines of history, literary studies, philosophy, and theology as part of the Geisteswissenschaften (the cultural or moral sciences) in contrast to the Naturwissenschaften (the natural sciences).[10] The hermeneutic movement was particularly concerned to resist the naturalization of mind, that is, the modeling of mind after the objectifying sciences of the neurobiology, physiology, and physics of that era. To say it bluntly, the hermeneutic movement was a strategy in the humanities to counter what my New York University psychologist friend thought was certain to happen when he made his prediction in the early 1990s.

The hermeneutic movement had an interest in phenomenological description but primarily in the description of meaning housed in the great literary classics that were formative in shaping Western civilization. Phenomenology in the more rigorous sense of that term began with late-nineteenth-century German philosopher Edmund Husserl. Husserl, however, advocated a kind of transcendental phenomenology that pursued a stringent description of the objects of consciousness when both the presuppositions of the existence of the personal ego and assumptions about the existence of objects in the external world were bracketed, suspended, or set aside.[11]

Hermeneutic phenomenology is different from Husserl's transcendental reduction of both the existence of the objects of description and the perceiving and describing personal ego. Hermeneutic phenomenology should even be distinguished from William James's kind of phenomenological psychology, which allowed the personal ego and its unique experiences as legitimate subject matter for phenomenological description.[12] Husserl was too influenced by Descartes for my taste. He, like Descartes, founded epistemology on the pure ego that had been stripped of its linguistic and historical constitution. Early in his career, Ricoeur had published profound transcendental phenomenological studies of the essence of the will in *Freedom and Nature* (1966) and the fallibility of the will in *Fallible Man* (1965).[13]

But when Ricoeur decided he wanted to study the actual experience of human fault, in contrast to the mere possibility of fault, he turned to hermeneutic phenomenology and studied the epigenetic history of the Western symbols and myths of fault and evil in his monumental *Symbolism of Evil* (1967).[14] The presupposition of this turn from pure phenomenology to hermeneutic phenomenology was the conviction that from the beginning the ego could not be the pure ego of Descartes and Husserl. It was, instead, both an embodied ego located in a desiring body and an ego constellated by language, tradition, and symbols from our inherited cultural past.[15] We are feeling and desiring creatures who project our feelings through mediations of linguistic metaphors and symbols.

This is why Ricoeur, as do metaphor and cognitive theorists George Lakoff and Mark Johnson,[16] believes that philosophy should anchor itself in the deep avowals and confessions of human consciousness that express themselves in metaphors and symbols.[17] As Ricoeur wrote: "The symbol gives rise to thought" (Le symbole donne à penser).[18] By this he means that philosophy, and by implication psychology, studies a human consciousness and unconsciousness that are mixtures of desire constellated, however vaguely, by the great metaphorical and symbolic resources that have formed a cultural tradition. If this is true, there is hardly any way that either philosophy or psychology can avoid the subjects of spirituality and religion. These symbols and narratives from our various cultural traditions already have in some way shaped the minds of both the psychological investigators and the subjects they study and try to heal.

So, Ricoeur's hermeneutic phenomenology starts not in describing pure consciousness, as does Husserl's, but in describing the embodied consciousness shaped by the metaphors, symbols, myths, and narratives mediated by interpersonal, social, and cultural traditions. But before we review how he brings into his hermeneutic description the distanciating and explanatory interests of the natural sciences, we need to learn a bit more about how hermeneutic phenomenology works. Hermeneutic phenomenology has four core ideas.

The first core idea is Gadamer's important theory of "effective history," a concept that Ricoeur freely appropriates.[19] This idea points to the situated character of all thinking and investigation. Historical texts, events, and monuments are not simply things that linger in the past and have no effect on us today. The past is mediated to us today and shapes us in myriad ways that we often cannot name or easily bring to consciousness.

Second, this effective history shapes what Gadamer called our "pre-understanding." These pre-understandings are the inherited frameworks that we rely on when attempting to understand our experience of the world, especially that which has already shaped us.[20] We would not understand our everyday experience if we did not have this fund of interpretive frameworks accumulated through repeated successful understandings of past generations. From one perspective, these pre-understandings function like prejudices, but from another perspective they are comparative references that make sense of our experiences. They may need to be tested and, as I will argue, both science and religion can play a very important role in testing and refining some of these pre-understandings of our inherited cultural, spiritual, and religious traditions. But these pre-understandings from our effective histories should not be denied and suppressed, as more positivistic philosophy and science are inclined to do. They serve a purpose, and they cannot be tested if they are not interpreted and understood. Such testing and interpretation is part of the task of religious humanism and, as I will argue, both philosophy and the various psychologies can contribute much to this testing process.

The third concept is about the most basic character of all human understanding. From the perspective of hermeneutic phenomenology, all understanding is like a dialogue or a conversation.[21] In fact, understanding *is* a dialogue and conversation. The structure of a dialogue is an ontological feature of human consciousness. Understanding anything—be it a past or present event, a behavior, a conversation, a therapeutic exchange, a spiritual exercise, or a ritual process—is first of all a matter of dialogue. This may sound trivial, but the point is profound, especially when making this assertion to scientists. It is asserting, in effect, that understanding something is not first, and not fundamentally, an objective process. This claim is often difficult for scientists to comprehend, but this is precisely what the Richardson team and Philip Cushman are contending in their respective books reinterpreting the entire range of psychology and psychotherapy as hermeneutic disciplines.

The fourth concept is closely associated with the idea of all understanding as dialogue. It makes an important tie between understanding as dialogue and the nature of moral thinking. Gadamer and Ricoeur believe that moral interests shape the understanding process from the beginning. This means that we do not first determine the objective nature of experience and the world and then determine how to apply this objective knowledge to concrete situations of moral action, even when these situations take the form of therapeutic interventions or care. Gadamer says it well when he writes: "We, too, determined that application is neither a subsequent nor a merely occasional part of the phenomenon of understanding, but co-determines it as a whole from the beginning."[22] By using the word *application* in this passage, Gadamer means practical moral application. This is my favorite passage from Gadamer. It asserts that there is an unbreakable tie between understanding and practical moral reason. Understanding can never be totally neutral nor objective; our practical interests and pre-understandings will always enter into the picture, shaping understanding from the very beginning.

The Role of Objectivity or Distanciation

I can imagine by now that many of you are becoming nervous. Isn't science about objectivity, explanation of causes, controlled observations, and, if possible, experimentation so that variables can be controlled and manipulated? And, of course, the answer must be yes. These are legitimate interests of science, and they make science what it is. This leads me to advocate not only a hermeneutic phenomenology as a beginning point for both philosophy and psychology but a particular version of that point of view called *critical hermeneutics* or *hermeneutic realism*. This view is also associated with the hermeneutic philosophy of Paul Ricoeur in contrast to the hermeneutics of Gadamer and his teacher Martin Heidegger. Critical hermeneutics finds a place for explanation and the kind of epistemological distance that we mistakenly call objectivity.[23] In other words, Ricoeur's view of hermeneutics finds a place for what we call science. But for him, and for me, the explanatory and distancing objectives of science do not stand on their own foundation. They evolve out of a prior understanding of the effective history that shapes us all and then returns to that history with refinements and adjustments to the massive funds of wisdom and insight that tradition delivers to us from the tested, and sometimes not-so-tested, experience of the past.

Ricoeur is actually critical of Gadamer for his neglect of science in his dialogical view of human understanding. In his book *Hermeneutics and the Human Sciences* (1982), Ricoeur suggests that the very title of Gadamer's magnum opus reflects a neglect of science. He writes: "The question is to what extent the work deserves to be called *Truth AND Method*, and whether it ought not instead to be entitled *Truth OR Method*."[24] By the word *method*, Ricoeur is referring to Gadamer's neglect of the role of distanciation and causal explanation in the larger framework of understanding. Gadamer, Ricoeur explains, was so concerned with what he called "alienating distanciation" (Verfremdung) and its influence on disconnecting modern consciousness from tradition that he unfortunately neglected science and explanation altogether.[25] Gadamer's concern has been transmitted to Frank Richardson and his team, who see the alienation of modern consciousness from tradition wrought in part by scientific psychology and psychotherapy as resulting in a kind of "ontological individualism" that gives "primacy to individual self-fulfillment," dissociated from the wisdom and claims of tradition.[26]

To counter this neglect of science in a hermeneutic model of human understanding, Ricoeur proposes substituting the concepts of distanciation and diagnosis for the concept of objectivity.[27] To illustrate the meaning of these concepts, one can turn to the way a medical doctor or even a psychotherapist might use the more scientific diagnostic tools of her profession—in medicine, the blood pressure monitor, stethoscope, x-ray machine, or CT (CAT Scan), or in psychology, the DSM-IV, TAT, Rorschach test, any number of pencil and paper tests, or even PET, SPECT, or the fMRI. The use of such instruments for diagnostic purposes generally will be preceded by an interview—indeed a conversation—about how the subject feels, thinks he feels, thinks is right or wrong with his functioning, work life, marital life, or friendships. According to Ricoeur, what the physician and psychologists learn from the objective instruments gains its meaning significantly with reference to the embodied subjectivity, lived experience, and encoded effective history of the patient or client.

With this illustration in mind, we can comprehend how to envision explanation as not pure objectivity without presuppositions but degrees of distanciation that make sense only in relation to describing a more basic foreground of social and historical experience, belonging, and embeddedness. Hence, rather than celebrating either extreme—the pretensions of objective science or Gadamer's uncritical embeddedness in tradition—Ricoeur asks: "Would it not be appropriate . . . to reformulate the question in such a way that a certain dialectic between the experience of belonging and alienating distanciation becomes the mainspring, the key to the inner life, of hermeneutics?"[28]

Hence, for Ricoeur, truth—which he identifies with the hermeneutic understanding of the effective history that has formed us—and scientific method and explanation are not viewed, as they are for Gadamer, as a matter of either-or. Rather, he sees truth and scientific method as "a dialectical process."[29] I must point out, however, that it is precisely the act of including explanation as a submoment of understanding that turns hermeneutic phenomenology into critical hermeneutics of the kind that I am advocating. In this model, the task of explanation is important and in some instances can contribute refinement and critique to the great fund of inherited wisdom (as we will see in chapter 2 and throughout my later arguments).

This is the epistemology that I believe should guide the dialogue between science and religion, especially the dialogue between religion and the psychological scientific disciplines. This is the model that will bear the most fruit in studying human consciousness, its preconscious or unconscious depths, forms of healing and psychotherapy, the analogues between psychotherapy and spirituality, or the processes of moral and spiritual development. This is also the model I recommend for reviving both religious humanism in general and Christian humanism in particular. An epistemology that prioritizes understanding over explanation leads one to take the effective history of the past with the utmost seriousness. It provides models of consciousness, prototypes of intervention, and traditions of confession, restoration, and healing that the modern disciplines may be able to refine but not completely invent. Science will move more firmly and successfully into the future if it also keeps in touch with the past.

Beginning with the Traditions That Form Us

I have confessed already that I will illustrate many of my arguments with the tradition I know best—the Christian tradition. This is not just a confession of my own limitations but a strategy that a critical hermeneutical phenomenology itself also demands. Because of the massive influence of Christianity on the institutions, cultures, and effective history of the West, this tradition—in its interaction and absorption of elements of Judaism, Greek philosophy, and Roman and German law—constitutes an important part of the effective history and consciousness of vast numbers of people, even those who do not profess this religion or any religion at all. The dialogue between science and religion, or between religion and the psychological disciplines, should not neglect this tradition of understanding.

This message is especially relevant to the new movement of positive psychology. Of all the movements in psychology today, it has returned to a vital dialogue with the traditions of the past for inspiration, new hypotheses, and the possible refinements that science can offer. One can see this trend in Jonathan Haidt's well-received *The Happiness Hypothesis: Finding Modern Truth in Ancient Wisdom* (2006).[30] Throughout this engaging summary of many of the advances in positive psychology, Haidt is constantly referring to the treasures of the great religious and philosophical traditions of the world, especially Buddhism, because of its sophisticated philosophical psychology.

The psychologically literate philosopher Owen Flanagan, although not a positive psychologist, used the fruits of that field extensively in his recent

Templeton Lectures titled *The Really Hard Problem: Meaning in a Material World* (2007).[31] But he, like Haidt in his appropriation of the insights of the past, skips rapidly from the eudaimonism of Aristotle to his interpretation of the emphasis on mindfulness, nonsuffering, and human flourishing found in the texts of the Buddha and some of his philosophical followers.[32] In the process, Flanagan fails to trace the mixture of Aristotelian eudaemonism and Christianity that developed in the philosophical psychology of Thomas Aquinas, his followers, much of the Protestant Reformation, and the great tradition of Roman Catholic social teachings which has had so much influence on the human rights movement of the modern world.[33]

My point is that in reviving the tradition of religious humanism through a dialogue between science and religion, and between religion and psychology, we must not neglect the effective history of the West. At least some of us should be permitted to start in our own backyards. And if we do that, we will gain even more and firmer insights and then gradually expand our dialogue to include the rest of the world.

2

Broadening Psychology,
Refining Theology

In the first chapter, I suggested that the main accomplishment of the growing dialogue between science and religion, and between psychology and theology, was the possible stimulation of a renewed religious humanism. I claimed that the meeting ground of this new religious humanism would be a phenomenological attitude—in fact, a critical hermeneutical phenomenology—practiced on the part of both science and religion. I did not propose banishing either causal explanations in science or metaphysical speculation in philosophy, theology, or science, but I counseled a stance of humility and patience that would restrain prematurely dogmatizing either of these cognitive stances.

I also revealed my belief that both science and religion—indeed, both psychology and theology—would profit from this dialogue and collaboration. For example, psychology would be broadened and theology would be refined. What do I mean by the two terms *broadened* and *refined*? I mean that psychology will develop new objects of study and new hypotheses to test, and that theology will receive refinements in its efforts to reconcile certain tensions, especially regarding its views about the rhythms of nature, that exist within complex traditions full of diversity and competing interpretations.

In this chapter, I primarily will illustrate what I mean by refining theology and then will address what that implies for broadening psychology. Let's first, however, turn to two examples—or case studies—on ways psychology can offer certain limited but important refinements to theology.

Spiritual Transformation and Atonement

Much of my work on the relation of psychotherapy and theology began many years ago. My first published book, titled *Atonement and Psychotherapy* (1966), addressed this subject. In that book, I tried to articulate the core elements of psychotherapeutic change and then use them as an analogy for interpreting and resolving tensions in the Christian doctrine of atonement, which has to do with the meaning and work of Christ's death on the cross.

My recent reading in comparative healing and the social neuroscience of psychotherapy gives me confidence that my early work may not be as dated as I feared. This feeling of encouragement came especially in reviewing the chapters in a volume titled *Spiritual Transformation and Healing* (2006), edited by anthropologist Joan Koss-Chioino and theologian Philip Hefner. Several of the chapters throw light on what Koss-Chioino calls the "core elements of the healing process," which can be found in both the folk healing rituals across many cultures and many manifestations of modern psychotherapy.[1] Basic to these core elements is what she and several other authors call "radical empathy."

In situations of Puerto Rican folk healing that Koss-Chioino has studied, radical empathy refers to the healer's deeply emotional and embodied understanding of and identification with the suffering, and the forces causing the suffering, of the ailing person. Indeed, the healer functions like a wounded healer, someone who has experienced such suffering, been cured, and then gone on to heal others. Because much of her study has taken place in the Puerto Rican situation of medium, patient, and community, the empathy she sees working is not limited to the individual seeker, the way empathy tends to function in the psychotherapeutic theories of Carl Rogers or Heinz Kohut. She calls it a radical empathy because it includes the seeker, the seeker's community, and the spirit powers, both good and evil, that have on some occasion afflicted them all—seeker, healer, and participating witnesses. Koss-Chioino believes the depth of empathy and self-identification of healer with seeker that occurs in such ceremonies makes radical empathy more like sympathy than the more boundary-respecting empathy advocated by Rogers and Kohut.[2]

A typical healing service takes place in a small room with one or more mediums sitting at a table, with thirty or so people in the audience. After readings and focusing meditations that get the mediums and audience in contact with their spirit worlds, the suffering individual comes to the table to dialogue with the medium. The medium has already made contact with the "spirit-cause of the attendee's distress."[3] Listen to how Koss-Chioino characterizes what happens next.

> A kind of probing by the medium ensues in which the indicated sufferer is queried as to his feelings—including physical complaints—and the circumstances in his life that may be causing him distress. The medium at this point has "captured" (*captar*) or formed (*plasmar*) within herself the inner experience of the sufferer, and she asks for verification from the sufferer (who replies affirmatively . . . approximately 97 percent of the time).[4]

The session moves to a resolution when the spirit causing the illness comes to the meeting and possesses another medium. The sufferer then enters into dialogue with the spirit-cause of his illness, and the other medium asks the spirit to leave and the sufferer to forgive the offending spirit. The spirit-cause, speaking through a medium, consents to leave, repents, accepts forgiveness, and is taken off the sufferer.

Radical Empathy in Neuroscience and Psychotherapy

Social neuroscientist Michael Spezio also uses the concept of radical empathy with reference to modern practices of medicine and psychotherapy. In these settings, he refers to an "ethics of therapy" that entails a method of emotional processing by the therapist that occurs in an intersubjective and narratively conveyed communicative exchange with the client that will entail new experiences and emotional transformation of them both.[5] What Spezio means by the therapist's "emotional processing" is close to what the Rogersian Eugene Gendlin meant by how empathy enhances new experiencing of the client's poorly acknowledged buried emotions, an experiencing that may be the key to therapeutic change.[6] It is also close to what attachment therapist David Wallin, following Peter Fonagy, likes to illustrate with the Buddhist concept of "mindfulness"—a reflective attitude toward present experience that helps the client own and symbolize what attachment therapists sometimes call the "unthought known."[7] Spezio uses simulation theory to develop his point. He writes: "*Simulation theory* advances the notion that the emotional processing involved in one's own bodily states is also required for the accurate judgment of others' emotional states, via a partial simulation of these states within the person doing the judging."[8] He even goes on to specify some of the areas of the brain involved in this emotional processing. He writes:

> Abundant evidence has revealed that several key brain areas that either are required for healthy emotional experience or are differentially activated by emotional conditions are also required for healthy social judgment. . . . The areas that most consistently show this association are the ventromedial prefrontal cortex, the right insula and somatosensory cortices . . . , and the amygdala.[9]

Of course, activating emotional processing in both client and therapist facilitates not only understanding but also recognizing and assimilating new experiences and insights valuable for therapeutic change. This is why both psychotherapy and the folk healing discussed by Koss-Chioino see narrative as so facilitating to emotional processing. Spezio defines narrative, or story, as a structured retelling of an experience that is freighted with emotions about goals, plans, expectations, failures, and perhaps solutions. The "minding" of other and self in the therapeutic process requires the following: "listening to a narrative as an other tells it is an active, embodied process, one that benefits from and can contribute to a sympathetic healer-seeker relation."[10]

Mediating the Theories of Christ's Death

Even though Koss-Chioino and Spezio deal with the seemingly different areas of folk healing and modern psychotherapy, their work on radical empathy has stimulated me to take another look at work I once did on how insights from psychotherapy could refine tensions in Christian understandings of the meaning and function of Christ's death and resurrection. As I indicated above, this is generally understood as the Christian theory of the atonement. The link between these two bodies of material is the simple observation that in both cases—the Christian theory of the cross as well as the work by Koss-Chioino and Spezio—the healer is emotionally moved and suffers and that this in itself contributes to overcoming brokenness.

In my early work, I primarily used the views of Carl Rogers on therapeutic empathy as well as analogues to these views found in Freud, Adler, Karl Menninger, the daseinanalysis of Medard Boss, and the family therapy team of Whitaker and Malone.[11] Today I could buttress these sources with the work of Heinz Kohut and the newly developing links between John Bowlby's attachment theory and psychotherapy found in the work of David Wallin and others.[12] But none of these sources had a full theory of emotional processing of the kind developing today in the social neurosciences by such scientists as Spezio and my University of Chicago colleague Jean Decety.[13] These advances, I think, justify revisiting my early work on how psychology can inform theology.

On atonement theory, I followed Gustav Aulén's typology in his masterful book *Christus Victor* (1961).[14] Aulén grouped atonement theories into Classic, Latin, and Moral or Modern. This typology is commonly regarded as a roughly valid guide to the most prominent constructive alternatives that the history of Christian thought has to offer on the subject of the meaning and work of Christ's death. The Classic or Christus victor view was so named because Aulén believed that it was most typical of the view found in the New Testament and the early Christian fathers. It is characterized as a continuous work of God (the supreme creator and healer) where God enters through Christ into the concreteness of human existence, identifies with this broken existence, takes the evil of this existence into God's very being, struggles with the superhuman forces of evil (not unlike the spirit-causes in Koss-Chioino's study), and eventually emerges victorious, liberating believers from the grip of these powers.

The Latin view, best illustrated by St. Anselm (1033–1109 A.D.) in *Cur Deus Homo*, was characterized by an understanding of Christ's death as a payment that restores God's honor and moral seriousness, that is, God's demand that humans live the righteous life that they were created to live.[15] According to this view, God's moral seriousness demands that humans be punished for their waywardness. But in forgiving humankind and restoring humans, instead of punishing them directly, God takes God's own retribution into God's self through the crucifixion of God's beloved son Jesus. It is in Christ's death that God's honor is defended, and it is in God's resurrection that the forgiveness of sins is symbolized and enacted. The so-called Latin view was dominant in much of medieval Roman Catholicism as well as in European and American Calvinism. It is what many Christians and non-Christians alike today believe is the only real and true meaning of Christ's death and resurrection.

But there has been a more modern, and indeed gentler or more benign, view of the atonement: the so-called Moral Influence view. This is an interpretation saying that Christ's death is chiefly an example of how humans ought to live. In Christ's death, God shows forth God's love for all humankind. This love is to be a new law and to arouse in us a similar kind of sacrificial and enduring love. This view is often called a subjective view; the change it brings is primarily in humans affected by the example of Christ. The other views are called objective because changes occur in God as well as in humans. In the Classic view, God in Christ undergoes the violent hostility and resistance of the spirit-powers that captivate and subject humankind. But in this view, God also remains consistent, engages with the struggles and frailties of humans, and, because of an enduring and unbreakable relationship with suffering humans, finally emerges victorious over the forces of evil. In the Latin view, the objective perspective is seen in the fact that God's moral honor is satisfied and upheld by an act of God; the penalty is extracted from God's own son, with whom God is fully identified in the incarnation.

Psychotherapy and the Atonement

In my early work, I thought that the Classic view was the more authentic, for two reasons. Like Aulén, I thought it was most consistent with the earliest witnesses in the New Testament texts and the writings of the early church fathers. But there was another reason. It seemed the most consistent with the general experience of healing human brokenness. It was better in articulating, albeit in ancient and mythological language, the role of embodied engagement of healer with sufferer and the sense of helplessness of many sufferers that is phenomenologically experienced as being possessed by powers over which they have no control.

In my comparison between the dynamics of psychotherapy and theories of the atonement, I turned to what was available and prominent during the 1960s. This was the work of the University of Chicago's Carl Rogers, who,

I think, is still influential but far less prominent than he once was. Many of his ideas have been so widely absorbed that they have lost their identity with his name. Although some of his theories are in many ways out of date, especially with regard to his understanding of the psychodynamics of human development, allow me to illustrate my argument with reference to his theories of psychotherapeutic change. I do this with added confidence since social neuroscientists Specio and Decety both honor Rogers's contributions to understanding therapeutic empathy.

At least three concepts explain Rogers's mature theory of the core elements of psychotherapy. The first is the concept of congruence. Rogers said that a good psychotherapeutic relationship occurs when the second person, whom he called the therapist, is congruent in the relationship.[16] Congruence means that the therapist in principle is able to have conscious access to all of her feelings and experiences, including her experiencing of the client's words and emotions, and to integrate them into conscious symbolization. Or, to say it differently, in order for the therapist to understand the client, her feelings about the relationship and the information she is receiving from the client must make contact with the roots of psychological life—what Rogers called "organismic experiencing." I think this is close to what Specio has in mind by simulation and what attachment therapist David Wallin means when he employs the Buddhist concept of "mindfulness."[17] The concept of congruence always seemed a bit too romantic to me in those days, even when I wrote admiringly about it. It is quite clear now, however, that this was Rogers's rather global and imprecise way of talking about what we just heard social neuroscientist Michael Spezio refer to as embodied emotional processing or simulation. When Rogers told us that organismic experiencing by the therapist was crucial for understanding the words and feelings of the client, he was close to saying what Spezio meant when he wrote that "several key brain areas that either are required for healthy emotional experience or are differentially activated by emotional conditions are also required for healthy social judgment."[18]

The second crucial element of a psychotherapeutic relationship is empathy. When recently I heard the new cognitive scientist at my university—University of Stockholm–trained Jean-Pierre Decety—give a lecture on the social neuroscience of empathy, I could not resist telling him that he was at the right school to study that subject. From the 1950s to the 1970s, the University of Chicago had been the great empathy university, since two of the leading theoreticians and practitioners of therapeutic empathy—Rogers and Kohut—had been members of its faculty during much of that period. Only a few decades before that, the philosopher George Herbert Mead packed classrooms by lecturing on the importance to social interaction of internalizing the other's point of view.[19] But Mead probably never fully comprehended what we now know about the somatic and neurophysiological processes undergirding the possibility of this so-called internalization process.

Here I primarily will describe Rogers's sometimes flat-footed way of emphasizing the importance of the therapist's capacity to take the lead in the emotional processing of linking symbolization and experience—what is said with what is felt—in the client's communication. Rogers defined empathy as a process of perceiving "the internal frame of reference of another with accuracy, and with the emotional components and meanings which pertain thereto, as if one were the other person, but without ever losing the 'as if' condition."[20] The "as if" qualification meant that Rogers wanted to respect the cultural individualism of Western societies. He avoided using the word *sympathy*, which Spezio prefers. And the radical empathy of Koss-Chioino would have frightened him. Nor would he have felt comfortable in the more undisciplined and spontaneous group settings of Koss-Chioino's Puerto Rican healing sessions. But he was on to something when he said this empathy should capture both the "emotional components and meaning" of the client's communication. Rogers was capturing an insight that has proved useful for studying spiritual transformation around the world, well outside the stage and structure of the psychotherapeutic hour.

The third element of this core is the following. In showing empathy, Rogers believed the good therapist would try to understand, feel, "prize,"[21] and even show "unconditional positive regard"[22] for all the emotionally toned communications of the client, even the negative or hostile ones, and even when these were aimed at the person of the psychotherapist. But why would a client ever become resistant, negative, or hostile toward the empathic and prizing therapist? The answer: because the therapist in her congruence is willing to feel and symbolize aspects of the client's experience that the client himself resists. But why would the client defend, sometimes angrily, against bringing into fuller awareness feelings and new experiences he actually is having? According to Rogers, it is because the client, through his socialization, has allowed his own energies of health and actualization to become diverted by inauthentic "conditions of worth"[23]—Rogers's term for false and absolutized values that judge and accuse the client, block feelings from awareness, and even function like the quasi-independent spirit forces of Koss-Chioino's Caribbean healing sessions. The key to healing, as Rogers's colleague Eugene Gendlin insisted, was the mutual "experiencing" of meaning and emotion that the therapist's congruent empathy and prizing facilitated, especially when it was consistent, steadfast, and unconditional.[24] This made it possible for the client to bring more fully into the center of awareness, symbolization, and emotional processing certain feelings and meanings that his own conditions of worth had pushed aside and made inaccessible. This was both a liberating experience for the client as well as a "moment of change," to use Rogers's phrase, toward greater degrees of integration and wholeness.

Radical Empathy and the Classic View of Atonement

When turning to the Classic *Christus Victor* understanding of the work of Christ's suffering on the cross, Aulén gives both biblical and early Christian evidence that it is more authentic than either the Latin or more modern Moral Influence view. I believe that Rogers's and Gendlin's view of the role of empathy and experiencing in therapeutic change also gives insights into the power of the Classic view. But Koss-Chioino's and Spezio's radicalization of empathy gives even more reason to see the Classic view as more profound than either the Latin or the Moral Influence view.

The relevant biblical evidence often clusters around the many portraits of Jesus' ministry as an engagement with, battle against, and final victory over the demons, principalities, and powers holding humans in bondage. The engagement with and casting out of spirit-forces in the case of the epileptic boy (Matt. 17:14-21), the Canaanite woman's daughter (Matt. 15:21-28), the dumb demoniac (Matt. 9:32-34), and the Gerasenes wild man (Mark 5:1-13 and Luke 8:26-33) were all healed by an act that engaged, sometimes named, and liberated these persons from the power that possessed them.

But these acts of liberation are depicted not so much as powerful acts of magic as acts of servanthood and suffering participation: "Just as the Son of Man came not to be served but to serve, and to give his life a ransom for many" (Matt. 20: 28). Aulén contends that there is additional evidence in the writings of Paul about the true meaning of Christ's crucifixion. He holds that such phrases as "for our sake," "in our stead," or "our Passover sacrificed for us" (1 Cor. 5:7) should be interpreted within the Christus victor motif of seeing God in Jesus entering into human experience and contending on our behalf against the spirit-powers of this world, even at cost of great suffering on his part due to their resistance, attacks, and hostility. [25]

Irenaeus, the second-century bishop of Lyons, may have been the leading systematic conveyor of the Christus victor view of Christ's ministry, suffering, and death. He interpreted both the incarnation of God in Christ and the crucifixion as a way of identifying with the fallen condition of humanity. Christ saved humans by participating in and recapitulating into his own life humankind's fallen and distorted existence. In communicating the meaning of this recapitulation, Irenaeus used several dramatic images that remind one of the dynamics of both empathy and radical empathy. He describes Jesus' life, suffering, and death as a matter of "stooping low,"[26] as a matter of being made "the very same thing"[27] as humans, and as a process of becoming "flesh," of putting "upon Himself the burden of man's sin," of putting "Himself in our position,"[28] and of taking upon himself "our infirmities" and "our ills."[29] All of this requires participation, struggle, steadfastness, and endurance in face of the enmity and resistance of the spirit-forces that both judge and bind human beings.

Do the concepts of empathy in Rogers or the idea of radical empathy as developed by Koss-Chioino and Spezio offer an illuminating analogy by which to understand this ancient story? And do these ideas help us refine the tensions among the Classic, Latin, and Moral Influence views on the meaning of Christ's ministry, death, and resurrection? I think they do. They at least give rise to a hypothesis requiring further research and analysis. Both empathy and radical empathy convey the idea that the healing of spiritual human brokenness—whether it be called neurotic bondage to our conditions of worth or possession by spirit-forces—is best overcome through therapeutic participation, simulation, and deep somatic processing of the experience of the broken person. In the case of radical empathy, this can sometimes entail an empathy for a larger group and a series of healings as it did in the groups Ross-Chioino studied. We learned from Rogers and Gendlin that empathic understanding needs to be a matter of organismic experiencing, not just an intellectual reflection of the client's or seeker's words. Social neuroscience may give us even more accurate concepts to understand the process.

But the healer's bodily identification with the seeker, in both modern therapy and some examples of folk healing, leaves us with at least this additional thought. Was the history of the Christian tradition on to something important in its insistence that in Christ's bodily identification with humankind in his suffering, and his death, there was the bodily and healing presence of the sacred as well?

It is probably easy for many modern readers to see the deeper truth of the Christus victor model in contrast to the Latin model. But what about the more modern Moral Influence view of Christ's suffering and death?

Why isn't the example of Christ's suffering love sufficient or finally true? Why must we worry with either the mythological language of suffering love overcoming the powers of evil *or* the juridical language of honor and payment?

One thought on this question is all that space permits me to convey. In the Moral Influence model, there is no emotional exchange, no actual participation in our captivity and suffering, no empathy into our world of estrangement and alienation from the source of all genuine relationships. It is an example, a model viewed from a distance, and an act of self-giving seen from afar. In the Moral Influence view, there is no deep participation and communication of the kind that brings suffering and change to both seeker and healer. In light of what we have learned about healing change from the modern sciences, maybe we once again should entertain the wisdom of the ancient classical Christus victor interpretation of the meaning of Christ's love, ministry, suffering, death, and endurance in the resurrection.

Notice, however, the essence of my argument. I have not said insights from psychotherapeutic empathy can correct or maybe even end in rejecting Christian views of the meaning of Christ's death. I have contended instead that with regard to the ongoing conversation within Christianity over these different views, insights from psychotherapy, anthropology, and social neuroscience may help *refine* this dialogue and show ways in which one perspective may indeed capture dynamics of human change with more sensitivity than another and yet still be faithful to the central witness of the tradition.

Another Example: The Agape, Caritas, and Eros Debate

A more concrete example will help demonstrate that the current dialogue between science and religion can contribute refinements to religion and offer new hypotheses and a more generous epistemology to science. I will use the example of the Christian understanding of love. What is

Christian love? Most people know that love is very central to the Christian religion. The Christian God is represented as a God of love. Jesus is said to love all humanity, so much so that he was willing to bear the cross for our sake.

But what does this really mean, especially for the love that individual Christians are to exhibit in their practical lives? There are many different interpretations of Christian love. Different branches of Christianity conflict over varying interpretations of Christian love. Since that is true, is it pretentious to suggest that science might make certain refinements to our understanding that might throw light on these competing interpretations? And might scientific moral psychology gain new hypotheses for research into moral and spiritual development by becoming acquainted with this inner Christian debate? I think the answer to both of these questions is yes.

Three major tensions mark theological discussions of Christian love. They center around the Greek words *agape* and *eros* and the Latin word *caritas.* A famous book titled *Agape and Eros* (1953), written by Swedish theologian Anders Nygren, traced the debate through Christian history.[30] Nygren believed that the truly normative and authentic understanding of Christian love is found in the word *agape,* the Greek word used for Christian love in the New Testament. He thought it refers to a kind of self-giving and self-sacrificial love that is possible only by the grace of God.[31] Nygren was particularly interested in arguing that Christian love did not build on the love that Greek philosophers called *eros.* He claimed that the term *eros* refers to the natural desires of humans to have and unite with the goods of life. This includes the goods of health, wealth, affiliation, and pleasure, but it also includes the higher goods of beauty and truth. Nygren's point, however, was that Christian love does not build on or incorporate eros—the natural aspirational strivings of humans. He believed he found this agapic view of Christian love in the New Testament (especially the writing of the Apostle Paul) and in Martin Luther, the giant of the Protestant Reformation.

Nygren was particularly interested in dismantling the classical medieval Roman Catholic view of Christian love, which was often summarized with the word *charity* or the Latin word *caritas*. Why did Nygren oppose the caritas view of Christian love? He did so because the meaning of love as caritas did exactly what Nygren thought Paul and Luther, his theological heroes, did not do. Love as caritas is built on, or at least includes, eros. Caritas in the Catholic view of Christian love included natural desires for health and affiliation but expanded these motives to a self-giving benevolence to others. All of this seemed too naturalistic for Nygren. It seemed to play down the importance of God's transforming grace. He joined other European neo-orthodox theologians of his day, such as Karl Barth and Rudolph Bultmann, in cutting off Christian love from natural eros.[32] This in effect was to disconnect Christian love from nature and desire—the very things scientists tend to study. Beginning with Nygren's strong view of agape and the strong supernaturalism of both Nygren and Barth, there was little room in these mid-twentieth-century Protestant trends for a productive dialogue between Christian ethics and the new scientific advances in moral psychology, evolutionary psychology, and neuroscience.

At the same time, however, breakthroughs in these very disciplines have led to a new reassessment of the Catholic caritas model of Christian love. But before I review in more detail how this model worked, especially in the thought of the great medieval Roman Catholic theologian Thomas Aquinas, let me first review some of the moral implications of insights into kin altruism and inclusive fitness emerging today from evolutionary psychology and social neuroscience.

Moral Implications of Kin Altruism and Inclusive Fitness

The idea of inclusive fitness was first put forth in 1964 by William Hamilton.[33] Hamilton's view of inclusive fitness holds that living beings struggle not only for their individual survival but for the survival of offspring and kin who also carry their genes. Their altruism initially is likely to be proportional to the percentage of their genes that others carry. This insight was further developed by the concept of parental investment, which Ronald Fisher and Robert Trivers (1972) defined as "any investment by the parent in an individual offspring that increases the offspring's chance of surviving . . . at the cost of the parent's ability to invest in other offspring."[34] These insights were at the core of the emerging field of sociobiology and were first brought to wider public attention by E. O. Wilson's book *Sociobiology: The New Synthesis* (1975).[35]

But the moral implications of the concepts of inclusive fitness, parental investment, and kin altruism have received competing interpretations. Richard Dawkins, in his *The Selfish Gene* (1976), turned these ideas into a defense of philosophical ethical egoism and argued that all altruistic acts are disguised maneuvers to perpetuate our own genes.[36] But there are other interpretations as well. Social neuroscientist John Cacioppo interprets our motives toward inclusive fitness and kin altruism as the core of human intergenerational care and the vital link between sociality and spirituality. In cooperation with his colleagues, Cacioppo's research on loneliness uses evolutionary theory on inclusive fitness to order many of his findings. From the perspective of this model of basic human motivations, loneliness can be seen as a condition that "promotes inclusive fitness by signaling ruptures in social connections and motivates the repair or replacement of these connections."[37] According to Cacioppo's interpretation of inclusive fitness, our gene continuity is not ensured simply by having our own children. Our children also must have children as well. And this is a challenge entailing long-term expenditures of energy. To account for this, Cacioppo writes something about human infant dependency that is very close to what both the Greek philosopher Aristotle and the medieval Roman Catholic theologian Thomas Aquinas set down many centuries earlier. Cacioppo writes:

> For many species, the offspring need little or no parenting to survive and reproduce. Homo sapiens, however, are born to

the longest period of abject dependency of any species. Simple reproduction, therefore, is not sufficient to ensure that one's genes make it into the gene pool. For an individual's genes to make it to the gene pool, one's offspring must survive to reproduce. Moreover, social connections and the behaviors they engender (for example, cooperation, altruism, alliances) enhance the survival and reproduction of those involved, increasing inclusive fitness.[38]

According to this view, the twofold interaction between inclusive fitness and the long period of infant dependency has shaped humans over the long course of evolution into the social and caring creatures we are. Sociality is a fundamental characteristic of humans, and, according to Cacioppo, spirituality in its various forms is an extension of sociality. Religion is generally, although not always, good for our mental and physical health—our heart, our blood pressure, our self-esteem, and our self-control—just as having good friends and family or not being lonely is also good for our well-being.[39] Cacioppo and colleagues do not equate sociality and religion; they are fully aware that religions are complex phenomena with many different doctrinal, ethical, ritual, organizational, personal, and social features that require rigorous experimental or clinical population studies to sort out how they affect human behavior, even from the perspective of how they influence the more limited goal of health. Nonetheless, Cacioppo seems to hold that the sociality that most religions offer is a key reason for their efficacy in human well-being.

Christian Love versus Health

My concern here is the topic of Christian love and not simply Christianity's contribution to mental and physical health. Although Jesus is said to have performed miracles of health, offering health in this world has never been at the core of Christianity or, for that matter, the other Abrahamic religions of

Judaism and Islam. Bringing to maturity loving and self-giving persons has been the primary concern of Christianity, whether or not this contributes to health and well-being. But the question is, as I elaborated above, Does Christian love build on eros—that is, on our strivings for health and other goods—or does it come exclusively from some supernatural source, as Nygren believes the normative tradition taught? And did Christianity ever identify eros and our deepest motivations with something like inclusive fitness and kin altruism?

Let me start with Aquinas. In the "Supplement" to his *Summa Theologica III,* Thomas follows Aristotle and the Roman natural-law theorist Ulpian in asserting that humans share with all animals an inclination to have offspring.[40] Having said this, he then introduces a very modern-sounding commentary on the uniqueness to humans of the long period of infant dependency. Notice the similarity of his argument to the earlier words of Cacioppo. Aquinas writes:

> Yet nature does not incline thereto in the same way in all animals; since there are animals whose offspring are able to seek food immediately after birth, or are sufficiently fed by their mother; and in these there is no tie between male and female; whereas in those whose offspring needing the support of both parents, although for a short time, there is a certain tie, as may be seen in certain birds. In man, however, since the child needs the parents' care for a long time, there is a very great tie between male and female, to which tie even the generic nature inclines.[41]

Although there is in this quote a description of how family formation emerges at the human level, there is an implicit argument for both the fact of human infant dependency and what we today call inclusive fitness. But these ideas are even more evident in the next quote, although stated very much from the male point of view, a habit typical of the time. Aquinas writes: "Since the natural life which cannot be preserved in the person of an undying father is preserved, by a kind of succession, in the person of the son, it is naturally befitting that the son succeed in the things belonging to the father."[42] Aquinas's main source for this insight was Aristotle's *Politics*. In one place, Aristotle wrote: "In common with other animals and with plants, mankind have a natural desire to leave behind them an image of themselves."[43]

However, in both Aristotle and Aquinas, such claims were not just about the importance of kin continuity; they were also statements about the origin and need of long-term investments by parents at the human level. In contrast to his teacher Plato, who, in his *Republic,* had advocated removing children from their biological parents in an effort to overcome the civil frictions created by nepotism,[44] Aristotle counters with an assertion about the origins of human care. Aristotle writes: "That which is common to the greatest number has the least care bestowed upon it." He believed that, in Plato's state, "love will be watery. . . . Of the two qualities which chiefly inspire regard and affection—that a thing is your own and that it is your only one—neither can exist in such a state as this."[45] This is an assertion about the importance of kin altruism in human care.

Although Aquinas saw these natural inclinations as important for forming long-term human care, he believed that they were not sufficient for mature parental love. Powerful social, cultural, and indeed religious reinforcements were also needed for stable parental investment to be realized. According to Aquinas, this, once again, is because of the many long years of human childhood dependency; human children need their parents for a very long time and through many contingencies and challenges. This leads Aquinas to develop his theology of marriage as a way of consolidating and stabilizing the commitment of parents—especially paternal commitment—to their dependent children.[46]

Although neither Aristotle nor Aquinas grasped the full intergenerational scope of Cacioppo's interpretation of kin altruism and inclusive fitness— that it must extend to our children's children and not just our own—both perspectives comprehended the interlocking nature of kin altruism and the wellspring of care, long-term human commitment, and hence some of the rudimentary energies of human sociality and morality. In other places, I have claimed that the concept of kin altruism as developed by evolutionary psychology and now social neuroscience can illuminate the motivational archeology of Erik Erikson's powerful concept of generative care.[47] But Erikson's idea of generativity includes not only long-term care for offspring but also the generalization of this care to nonkin and one's wider cultural work.[48] Erikson and Aquinas agree that the more expansive concern for and care of nonkin and the distant other springs from a generalization of a more intimate kind of altruism and kin attachments. Recent work by psychologist Michael Leffel insightfully has brought together Erikson on generativity, evolutionary psychology, and neo-Thomism for very insightful contributions to virtue theory and the redirection of contemporary research in the psychology of spirituality on how to conceptualize the ends of spirituality, shifting this research from an overemphasis on the ends of self-fulfillment and health to the generative activation of the strengths of both other and self.[49]

Of course, Aquinas, and those who followed him, supplemented these naturalistic observations with additional epistemological presuppositions that may seem strange to scientists. These included the idea that God works through nature as well as grace and hence that God is present in the kin altruistic inclinations of parents and grandparents. He also assumed that in order for kin altruism to be stable, the additional social reinforcements of marriage and, indeed, God's strengthening grace and forgiveness were needed.

In addition, he held—and Christianity has always taught—that Christian love includes more than kin altruism and the care of our familial offspring; it must include the love of neighbor, stranger, and enemy, even to the point of self-sacrifice. For the Christian, this was made possible by the idea that God was the creator of all humans and that hence each person was a child of God and made in God's image (*imago dei*). For this reason, as Kant would say on different grounds, each individual should be treated "always as an end and never as a means only."[50] In Aquinas's view, acting on this belief, and with the empowering grace of God, made it possible for Christians to build on and yet analogically generalize their kin altruism to all children of God—even those beyond the immediate family, their own children, and their own kin. These wider assumptions about the status of all persons as children of God may be beyond the competence of science to assess. They entail a step toward metaphysical speculation of the kind science might do better to avoid. Nonetheless, in this view of Christian love developed in Aquinas, the seeds of a religious humanism—in this case, a Christian humanism—began to form.

I have tried to illustrate how Aristotelian and Thomistic insights can join with insights from evolutionary psychology, social neuroscience, and Erikson's concept of generativity to refine debates over the Christian understanding of love. Here, I join the work of Stephen Pope and others in presenting this option.[51] The kind of Christian humanism found in Aquinas makes it possible for Christianity to be enriched by the modern sciences of human nature. Aquinas's view differs strikingly from Nygren's representation of Paul and Luther when he contends that Christian love does not build on our own natural energies but "has come to us from heaven."[52] Or again, it is very different from Nygren's view when he writes that the Christian is "merely the tube, the channel through which God's love flows."[53] It is stunning to observe the complete discontinuity in this statement between the downward love of God and the natural extension to nonkin of natural human kin-altruistic impulses. Such a view as Nygren's precludes the possibility of a religious humanism of the kind I have been describing. It eliminates the possibility of the refinements to religious views of human nature that the conversation between religion and science can offer.

My argument has been that a revived religious humanism can come about through the dialogue between religion and science, particularly between religion and the psychological sciences. I have illustrated this with the issue of love in Christianity. I believe my argument could be illustrated with other religions as well, especially the Abrahamic religions of Judaism and Islam. As Aristotle's influence created a kind of religious humanism in these religions in the past, the broader dialogue between science and religion may be able to do this for the future.

But the contributions will not simply flow from science to religion. Even in this short investigation, a question for science to investigate has arisen: How do religious and metaphysical concepts, such as the belief that all humans are children of God, work to extend the impulse of natural kin altruism, if at all? This goes beyond the issue of the relation of religion to health. It raises the question of the relation of religion to expansive love for the distant other. But this is an inquiry for another time.

Notes on My Personal Christology

I want to take this opportunity to bring together two sets of writings on Christology that can be found in my work over the years. My argument about the centrality of the Christus victor perspective on the meaning of Christ's life and death first appeared in *Atonement and Psychotherapy*, published in 1966. As the years rolled by, I began to ask questions about the relation of psychology and ethics. Related to that question was another one about the ethical implications of Christ's life and death. This latter question was especially important to clarify how the love expressed by Christ in his ministry and death functioned to illuminate the moral meaning of Christian love generally, particularly the love that individual Christians are to show forth in their lives.

Beginning with *Religious Thought and the Modern Psychologies*, and in several books after that, I elaborated a Christology aimed at clarifying the ethical and moral work of Christ's love and sacrifice.[54] This work was influenced by the neo-Thomist personalist and Roman Catholic moral theologian Louis Janssens as well as by various movements in theological feminism.[55] Janssens gives a Thomistic account of Christian love; he claims it should be understood with the caritas model summarized above in contrast to agape or eros. Janssens helps us understand an important issue pertaining to caritas: how the caritas that indeed builds on human natural inclinations also must be willing to perform acts of self-sacrificial love.

However, Janssens also affirms parts of Yale ethicist Gene Outka's somewhat Kantian view that Christian love should be interpreted as a sturdy form of mutuality or equal regard.[56] By this, Outka means that Christian love—indeed, the love shown forth by Christ—should be interpreted within the framework of the principle of neighbor love—"you shall love your neighbor as yourself" (Matt. 19:19). This is a command made several times throughout the Gospels and the Pastoral Epistles. It should be understood as well in close association to the highly analogous Golden Rule, which appears in Matt. 7:12 and Luke 6:31. For Janssens, these scriptural passages mean that "love of neighbor is impartial. It is fundamentally an equal regard for all persons, because it applies to each neighbor qua human existent."[57] He holds that this is true because each person is a child of God and redeemed by Christ and hence "of irreducible worth and dignity."[58]

Janssens follows the New Testament formulation of neighbor love, and also Kant, by saying that love as equal regard applies to both *other* and *self*. He insists that the impartiality of equal regard applies to the self as well as to other people. He believes that in accord with this impartiality, "we maintain that one is to have equal regard for self and for others, since the reasons for valuing the self are identical with those for valuing others, namely that every one is a human being."[59]

It is important to understand the unconditioned nature of Janssens's interpretation of Christian love. The mutuality of love as equal regard is not a matter of reciprocity. It is not conditioned by the response of the other. It is not a matter of if-then. It does not imply that I will love you *if* you love me. Love as equal regard does not cease loving the other in case the other does not respond or does not love in return. Loving the other and loving the self are predicated on the fact that both other and self are children of God and equally objects of God's love.

On the other hand, as is demonstrated in the case of Martin Luther King Jr.'s and Gandhi's doctrines of nonviolent resistance, love as equal regard does expect the other to learn to respect the selfhood of the loving resister; the resister's self merits this love just as does the other, even the oppressor. But the resister's love for the other is not conditioned on the return of love by the other; the love shown by nonviolent resistance continues all the same, as psychoanalyst Erik Erikson explains so well in his eloquent book *Gandhi's Truth* (1969).[60] Hence, love as equal regard *endures* even when rejected and hostilely attacked, and in the process of enduring it aspires to convert the other to show equal regard in return. This feature of the *endurance* of love even in the face of hostility is what brings love as equal regard into the orbit of the Christus victor interpretation of the atonement—the meaning of the sacrificial death of Christ.

Notice the logic of Janssens's position and the logic of much of what I have said over the past twenty years about the meaning of Christ's love and sacrifice. For Janssens, mutuality and equal regard point to the ideal of Christian love, and self-sacrificial love is derived from them. He writes: "Self-sacrifice is not the quintessence of love. . . . Self-sacrifice is justified derivatively from other regard" when other regard is viewed as a part of mutuality and equal regard. Hence, even when the community and mutuality of equal regard—not self-sacrifice as such—are the goals of Christian love, we must at times be willing to sacrifice some of our interests and actively expend energy on behalf of restoring a community of equal regard and mutuality once again. Janssens writes:

> After the model of God's love in Christ who loved us and gave himself up for us, our love is to include self-giving and self-sacrifice as long as we live in a world of conflict and sin. We should love our enemies and persecutors, take the initiative in forgiving, overcome evil with good, and even lay down our life for our friends.[61]

But, once again, we must be reminded that, according to this view, the Christian should pursue self-sacrifice not as an end in itself but as a transitional ethic toward the restoration and maintenance of true equal regard and mutuality.

There are at least two ways love as equal regard is synergistic with the Christus victor interpretation of the atonement. First, both views see Christ's love as principally an unconditioned, enduring, and unbreakable love for the other. Second, both views see Christ's love as a matter of an unqualified valuing of the worth of the other—a valuing that requires entering into the experiencing of the other. Loving the other in Janssens's neo-Thomistic view means not only treating the other as a rational end but regarding the other as a subject striving to realize the goods (what Janssens calls premoral goods) of life. To love the other, we must not only respect the other but actively work to realize the goods that the other needs to live a decent life. Hence, love as equal regard requires identifying with the experience of the other and the struggle to realize these goods, somewhat like the radical empathy of a therapist, a folk healer, and, at the cosmic level, Christ himself, which we saw both in some forms of psychotherapy and in the Christus victor view.

It is not my purpose here to completely close the distance between these two Christologies appearing in my work over time. I have been criticized in print for not linking the two Christologies.[62] Looking at the two from the vantage point of this moment in time makes me think that they can contribute to each other, especially the Christus victor view to the equal-regard model of Christian love. The equal-regard view has sometimes been criticized for seeing sacrificial love as a transitional moment rather than as an end in itself—a transitional moment designed to endure both sin and finitude until mutuality can be restored once again.[63] Although I reject this criticism for the reasons advanced above, I have developed in recent months some discomfort with one element of the equal-regard model of Christian love. Although I believe Janssens's view of love as equal regard is consistent with both the biblical witness and philosophical consistency, it does not sufficiently illuminate the dynamics of the transformative process that restores community and mutuality. Certainly, the relational steadfastness of both therapist and Christ amid the hostility and resistance of broken humanity points to a dimension of the transformative process. But the equal-regard Christology, in the way I developed it in the texts where ethics was my dominant concern, did not sufficiently attend to how love—even enduring love—actually transforms. Love as equal regard, whether articulated by either Janssens or my recent work, needs to incorporate insights about how empathy, radical empathy, the recapitulation of the broken person's suffering in the experience of the healer, and the therapist's experiencing of the client's denials can contribute to redemptive change. This would illuminate the relationships of all Christic figures—the good Christian, the good therapist, the folk healer of the wounded, or, at the cosmic level, Christ as God incarnate.

Christian love as equal regard has very important ethical implications for the task of a Christian moral theology. But it needs enrichment by the insights and dynamics of the Christus victor Christology. Or, to say it differently, the science-religion dialogue, when enriched by the insights of the transformative power of empathy and radical empathy, can actually help restore more fully a Christology that is simultaneously truly ethical and transformative.

Coda on Spirituality and Religion

I conclude with comments about the relation of spirituality and religion. The reader will notice that the word *spirituality* is in the title of this book but that the word *religion* is not. The reader may also observe that religion in its doctrinal and ethical forms seems much more the topic of this chapter than does spirituality.

Spirituality can be fruitfully defined as the relation of the self to what it considers to be transcendent or sacred.[64] Religion is a much broader concept that includes spirituality but also dimensions of community, ritual, ethics, doctrine, and social policy between religious communities and the outside world.[65] In this chapter, we have investigated what the dialogue between science and religion can contribute to the debate about conflicting doctrines of the atonement *and* to the controversy on the ethical meaning of Christian love—the tensions among eros, caritas, and agape. In both cases, my argument has been not so much that science can correct religious traditions as that scientific insights can help religious traditions refine and consolidate ongoing dialogues and controversies within their own history. This was the case when I argued that concepts of empathy and radical empathy could bolster the Classic view of the atonement in contrast to the Latin and Moral Influence views. This also was my argument when I contended that naturalistic insights into love could show the strength of the caritas view of Christian love in contrast to the eros and agape views.

But throughout these discussions, I was speaking about religion more than about spirituality in the narrow sense of that word. Religion always contains elements of spirituality, but the category of spirituality, both analytically and in actual practice, can function with very little attention to these broader features of ritual, shared communal practices, doctrine, ethics, or social teachings. This book argues for retaining the category of religion, in addition to spirituality, in the dialogue between science and religion. Some questions are best served by focusing on spirituality, but many other issues are even better advanced by keeping in mind the richness of spirituality when embedded in the fullness of religious institutions, traditions, and practices.

I will try to illustrate my point. Pastoral psychotherapist David Hogue has advanced some important points on this matter that I want to share. In brief, he argues that religious traditions, communities, shared rituals, ethics, and even doctrines reinforce, stabilize, and even deepen spirituality. Hogue argues that memory makes up a significant portion of the self's identity, even the self oriented around what it considers to be transcendent or sacred. This memory is largely made up of stories, collected and interpreted by the left hemisphere of the brain.[66] Following the narrative psychology of his Northwestern University colleague psychologist Dan McAdams, Hogue also believes that personal stories are adaptations of larger cultural narratives, pointing, I submit, to what Gadamer would call the profound "effective histories" of all selves.[67]

Hogue cites evidence that changes in the memories of the self, both conscious and unconscious, alter brain connections as well. This is true of even small changes in memory. Such changes, brought about by the retelling and reconstruction of personal stories, can occur in psychotherapy. But they also can occur in spiritual practices, especially spiritual practices that take place within the reinforcements of communities of worship, prayer, the study in groups of sacred texts, the introduction to and reinforcement of moral codes, and even the listening to religious exhortation such as sermons.[68] Furthermore, the liminality of ritual processes can loosen the boundaries of the self, thereby making it more open to change.[69] But when these liminal religious rituals take place in actual communities of faith, the self is more likely to be open to the wider ethics and doctrinal teachings of the group, hence effecting a more socially recognizable, and possibly even more classically tested, kind of change.

But we all know that religions can be demonic as well as beneficent. Even when spiritualities are embedded in structures of coherent communal traditions that help change to be even more far reaching, that in itself does not protect us from distorted and unproductive change. For this reason, spiritualities both within and outside embedded religious traditions need critique. Religious traditions contain ethics and morality. Furthermore, individualistic standing spiritualities have ethical attachments even if they are more or less disconnected from their original communities of origin. So, it is not enough to say that a psychotherapy, spirituality, or religious tradition produces change in the self, personality, or even the brain. Nor is it enough to say they contain implicit ethics of some kind. Every concrete practice of human change needs a metaethic of critique (an idea I will develop in chapter 3).

In conclusion, let me reassert that the dialogue between science and religion will be richer and will contribute more completely to the revival of religious humanism if it keeps in mind religion as well as spirituality. Furthermore, not only do all practices of change require an ethic and a metaethic, but the dialogue between science and religion, I will claim, can contribute substantially to both.

3

Change and Critique in Psychology,
Therapy, and Spirituality

At the end of chapter 2, I wrote that it is not enough for a spirituality, psychotherapy, or religious tradition to claim that it stimulates change in personality, character, or even the brain. As we saw in the U.S. presidential campaigns of 2008, appeals to change are popular and rhetorically effective but also sometimes conceptually vacuous. In fact, they can be so popular and rhetorically effective that all sides—liberal and conservative, establishment and nonestablishment, insiders and outsiders—can claim that they are the true agents of change.

But clear-headedness will soon teach us that claims to be able to change people or institutions tell us little about the kind of change being effected. Change can be good if it passes some critical tests concerning the good and the right. But how do we know when change is good and right? What are our criteria? By what standards do we judge change? Or, to use the language I used at the end of chapter 2, what should be our standards of critique?

The word *critique* is not frequently used to assess change in the context of psychotherapy or spirituality. It is more likely to be used in political theory, often in the context of Marxist or so-called Frankfurt school forms of thought designed to expose ideology, uncover injustice, and detect bias.[1]

The idea of critique is often associated with a Kantian-like move that uses Kant's categorical imperative to uncover class and racial distortion and forms of injustice. When I turn to the moral and political philosophy of Paul Ricoeur—which I will use extensively in this chapter and throughout the rest of the book—I will employ a dash of Kant myself in establishing a grounds for critique.

But I will also do something that Kant does not do and that Ricoeur probably does not do adequately. I will supplement my turn to Kant with a subordinate turn to the empirical. In this move, I will be influenced by the Principle of Minimum Psychological Realism (PMPR), a concept developed in the early works of the empirically oriented moral philosopher Owen Flanagan.[2] Although I will claim, as does Flanagan, that empirical research can throw only indirect light on the morally normative, it can illuminate the category of the premoral and the range of empirical realities within which moral action is both constrained and made possible. Along these lines, I will argue that appeals to the morally good should contain subordinate, premoral judgments about the goods of health, efficiency, sufficient wealth, and the smooth coordination of action. Hence, from my perspective, critique always should have both moral and premoral dimensions, that is, a place for both the moral sciences and the capacity of the natural sciences to illuminate the category of the premoral.

This chapter, as indeed this entire book, will reveal my indebtedness to William James. James is often cited as something of a hero by those contemporary scholars, such as Owen Flanagan, Jonathan Haidt, and Kwame Appiah, who believe that moral philosophy today must attend to the fruits of empirical moral psychology.[3] All three of these contemporary scholars believe, with James, that moral philosophy can gain insights into both moral norms and moral capabilities from scientific moral psychology. Princeton University professor of philosophy Kwame Appiah says it well in this historical narrative about the close association between psychology and philosophy that was the legacy of William James:

And the psychology labs at Harvard are in William James Hall because its inhabitants rightly think of James (who migrated from Harvard's Physiology Department to its Philosophy Department in 1881) as one of their ancestors, just as we contemporary philosophers claim him for ourselves. His colleague Josiah Royce was elected president of the American Psychological Association in 1902 and president of the American Philosophical Association in 1903.[4]

From my standpoint, it is not just James and a handful of his contemporary followers who are interested in bringing together psychology and normative disciplines such as moral philosophy. In contrast to the anti-empirical psychology mentality of Husserl and Heidegger, we must be reminded that Paul Ricoeur's hermeneutic realism always has been open to what empirical and clinical psychology can teach phenomenology about what he called the "archeology"—the deep empirical wellsprings—of the will and even the archeology of the symbol. This is why his great book *Freedom and Nature* (1966) is full of the best empirical psychology of his day in his effort to illuminate the involuntary, which was, as he taught, always in dialectical tension with the voluntary.[5] This respect for psychology led him to write his monumental book *Freud and Philosophy* (1970) in his effort to understand the naturalistic motives that both give rise to and are transformed in the symbolic process.[6] To carry this conversation between philosophy and the natural sciences further, Ricoeur late in his career consented to hours of dialogue with the famous French neuroscientist Jean-Pierre Changeux and recorded this conversation in their book *What Makes Us Think?* (2000).[7] As I pointed out in chapter 1, in contrast to most of his phenomenological colleagues, Ricoeur has always wanted to locate the place of scientific explanation, including psychological explanation, within the context of his larger hermeneutic phenomenological umbrella.[8]

The question before us, however, is how do we assess change, whether in the context of psychotherapy, spirituality, or other situations? I make the question all the more difficult because I assume that all change—even so-called psychological change—contains an implicit moral dimension, although it may be an inadequate moral dimension. I also will propose that philosophy, psychology, and even theology—or at least some form of religious narrative—have contributions to make to assessing and critiquing claims about change.

Earlier Sins and Preoccupations

Much of my earlier writing was preoccupied with assessing the claims about change in various schools of psychotherapy and counseling. My books *Generative Man* (1973, 1975), *The Moral Context of Pastoral Care* (1976), *Pluralism and Personality* (1980), and *Religious Thought and the Modern Psychologies* (1987, 2004) all were concerned with assessing and critiquing the images of human health and fulfillment implicit in many of the major schools of psychotherapy, pastoral psychotherapy, and pastoral counseling.

Some secular psychologists and pastoral counselors thought I was somewhat harsh in my moral analysis of the images of human fulfillment in the modern secular and religious therapies. In short, I found in their images of psychological health what I and other commentators, including Christopher Lasch, Philip Rieff, Martin Gross, Paul Vitz, and, more recently, Frank Richardson and his colleagues, saw as a kind of philosophical ethical egoism.[9] By philosophical ethical egoism, I meant a view of human health that put self-regard prior to other-regard and, in fact, made other-regard a derivative of self-regard. Sometimes this ethical egoism took a more explicitly hedonic form, as it did in the tension reduction theories of pleasure in Freud or the rationality goals of Albert Ellis.[10] Sometimes it took a more nonhedonic form, as in the self-actualization theories of Carl Rogers, Abraham Maslow, Fritz Perls, and Erich Fromm.[11]

Three observations may help justify, and perhaps excuse, the youthful excesses of my rather early, sour critiques. First, I always acknowledged that regaining a sense of initiative and self-regard was an important goal for both the secular and religious psychotherapies.[12] Human brokenness—whether conceptualized as neurosis, psychosis, or sin—entails an element of self-depletion and requires an outside agent or therapist giving empathy, warmth, positive regard, or grace to renew a positive sense of self-regard. It was because of my respect for the positive consequences of rehabilitated self-regard that I gravitated, as we saw in chapter 2, toward the caritas model of Christian love rather than the more demanding and self-denying strong agape model advocated by Nygren and, in a more modified form, even by Reinhold Niebuhr.[13]

My second excuse is this: the critique I advanced had less to do with the appropriate role of self-regard in the healing process itself and more to do with the tendency of the psychotherapeutic literature of the 1970s and 1980s to generalize health goals of change to more comprehensive cultural images of human fulfillment. In short, my criticism had to do with the subtle ways psychology and psychotherapy can feed cultural ideals. Philip Rieff's theory of "psychological man" stimulated my imagination. Rieff trusted Freud's controlled and skeptical ethical egoism more than he did humanistic psychology's or Jungian psychology's romantic and expressive form of egoism.[14] Although the cultural analysis of the psychotherapies that some of us did in those days has its legitimate place, I acknowledge the difficulty in getting busy clinicians to have much genuine concern about the larger cultural implications of their writings, research, and practice.

Third, in my book *Religious Thought and the Modern Psychologies* (1987)—especially the second edition (2004)—I introduced a distinction that I believe even today is highly relevant for properly evaluating both psychotherapeutic change and spiritual change.[15] This is the distinction that moral philosopher William Frankena made between nonmoral and moral goods or that Roman Catholic moral theologian Louis Janssens made between premoral and moral goods.[16] Throughout the first and second editions of that book, I argued that one main contribution of the modern psychologies and psychotherapies is their insight into the basic psychobiological needs and tendencies that make up the fundamental nonmoral or premoral goods of life—tendencies that humans should acknowledge, have access to, and in some way express if they are to live healthy lives. Health itself is a basic nonmoral or premoral good, as are wealth, knowledge, comfort, agency, and a raft of basic human skills.

But nonmoral or premoral goods are *not necessarily* fully moral goods. This is the insight that theories of psychotherapeutic change, and some theories of spiritual change, often overlook. We do not necessarily call the healthy, wealthy, knowledgeable, agentive, or skillful person a morally good person. This is because there can be conflicts between nonmoral or premoral goods; my claims for health may conflict with yours, my wealth may compete with yours, and my skills may displace yours.

I contend that *the moral good reconciles conflicting premoral goods,* both within the individual self and between self and others. The theoretical literature of some forms of psychotherapy moved too rapidly from their insights into the nonmoral or premoral good of health to the cultural and moral ideal of the morally good person. I will claim that health—psychological and physical—contributes to the morally good but does not exhaust the full meaning of the morally good.

With these three qualifications of my earlier excesses in mind, I would like to further refine my former interest in the critique of change. But to develop an even more mature discussion, I need a sophisticated pre-empirical theory of ethics and morality. To find such a theory, I propose turning to the model of ethics and morality set forth by Paul Ricoeur's challenging, but somewhat neglected, Gifford Lectures titled *Oneself as Another* (1992). It is in this text that Ricoeur sets forth the most complete statement of what he calls his "little ethics."[17]

Since the work of moral psychologist Lawrence Kohlberg, the field of moral psychology has recognized that it requires pre-empirical theories of ethics and morality to guide its empirical refinements. Kohlberg's choice of the cognitively oriented models of Plato and Kant advanced the field.[18] But it also led him to emphasize moral thinking in contrast to moral habits, virtues, or narratives and to model his understanding of morality after Kant's categorical imperative.[19] In other words, Kohlberg did his empirical research assuming that the most adequate form of morality was a form of moral thinking that follows a universal principle that treats the other as an end and never a means alone.

It is widely thought today that Kohlberg's brilliant insights into the need for a pre-empirical model of morality to guide empirical work led him to neglect the role of virtue, the place of narratives, the importance of premoral goods, and the reality and pressure of contexts and social situations. In turning to the model of ethics and morality put forth by Ricoeur, I hope to introduce a theory that finds a place for the elements that Kohlberg omitted without neglecting the importance of moral thinking and justice that he so profoundly understood.

Ricoeur's Model of Ethics and Morality

Although Ricoeur is a philosopher, his hermeneutic model of ethics and morality has great relevance not only to moral philosophy but also to moral theology, moral psychology, and any normative theory of change and fulfillment. His hermeneutic model of mature moral reflection and action both includes and yet is more than some of the standard models of morality presupposed by today's moral psychology.

Mature moral thinking and action, according to Ricoeur, develops along the following lines. He first makes a distinction between ethics and morality. In fact, he goes even further and asserts the temporal priority of ethics over morality in the full arch of moral reflection. In making this distinction, Ricoeur is echoing the distinction between nonmoral and moral, or, better yet, the distinction between premoral and moral. This is what Ricoeur means when he writes: "The present study will be confined to establishing the primacy of ethics over morality—that is, of the aim over the norm."[20] Or, to say it differently yet, Ricoeur is asserting the priority of the premoral (what he means by the term *ethics*) over morality.

Here is what he means. According to Ricoeur, the field of ethics springs from our desiring selves and from our efforts to realize some good—some premoral good—in our lives. Here is where Freud's theory of desire, humanistic psychology's view of the role of self-actualization and organismic experiencing, evolutionary psychology's view of the link between kin altruism and other-regard, and the new moral intuitionists' theory of moral emotions throw some light on moral development.[21] All of these perspectives cast some partial illumination on our premoral strivings and how they contribute to what Ricoeur calls the field of ethics. Morality, on the other hand, builds on, tries to fulfill, yet properly orders and critiques our ethical striving toward the premoral goods of life. In other words, morality assumes our ethical strivings toward the goods of life but also tries to adjudicate between conflicting expressions of the premoral good.

But how do we understand and learn about these aspirations toward the good? Do we learn about them by directly feeling and following our raw desires, actualization tendencies, and prereflective moral intuitions? Yes and no. Certainly, we have these emotions and feelings, but they are also always interpreted and tested by our inherited linguistic traditions and what they have learned over the ages about the true and lasting premoral goods of life. In answering this question about how we acquire knowledge of the premoral good, Ricoeur departs from the simplistic assumptions about the nature of experience found in much of modern psychology and psychotherapy. Ricoeur insists that rather than consulting our raw feelings or intuitions, we should instead try to *describe* our culture's and tradition's classic *practices* for pursuing these goods. Ricoeur writes: "The properly ethical character of these precepts is ensured by what Alasdair MacIntyre calls 'standards of excellence,' which allow us to characterize as good the practice of a doctor, architect, painter, or a chess player."[22] Such practices crystallize both our enduring premoral goods and the appropriate means to acquire them.

In emphasizing marks of excellence of our cultural practices as revealing the premoral goods of our ethical strivings, we see in Ricoeur shades of both the teleologically oriented modern psychologies and the communitarianism of Alasdair MacIntyre. This view says, in effect, that the goods of life are discovered not just intuitively through direct experience but also through the inherited practices of a community and its traditions.[23] Ricoeur accepts MacIntyre, up to a point, when the latter vividly illustrates the relation of goods and practices as follows:

> If, on starting to listen to music, I do not accept my own incapacity to judge correctly, I will never learn to hear, let alone to appreciate, Bartok's last quartets. If, on starting to play baseball, I do not accept that others know better than I when to throw a fastball and when not, I will never learn to appreciate good pitching let alone to pitch. In the realm of practices the authority of both goods and standards operates in such a way as to rule out all subjectivist and emotivist analyses of judgment. De justibus *est* disputandum.[24]

But teaching persons how to *describe* and act on the classic inherited practices of a tradition is, according to Ricoeur, just the beginning of ethics and just the first step toward the moral development or transformation of persons. It does not exhaust the full meaning of morality. Furthermore, the descriptive task itself is complex. If we are socialized beings at all, the more excellent forms of our desires are projected into a cultural tradition's hierarchies of linguistic codes that give intelligibility to our practices. These include codes of coordination (simple patterns of means to various ends), codes of subordination (such as plowing in order to farm), constitutive rules (such as moving the pawn to play the game of chess), plans of life (far-reaching goals and aspirations), images of the "good life" (general evaluative models as to what are truly valuable aspirations for life as a whole), and, finally, larger narratives that give unity and meaning to our life in the midst of the disappointments and conflicts.[25] All of these layers of language pattern our desires and practices at their very core, carry us toward more fully ethical action, and lead us to the doorstep of morality. They also require a great deal of description and interpretation by oneself, parents, educators, the wider community, and communities of faith in order to understand and appropriate them. Ethics understood as the pursuit of the premoral goods of life requires a grand and complex process of education, socialization, and critical interpretation on the excellent practices of a tested and established tradition.

Notice that "narration" was the last of the long list of ways that our practices seeking the goods of life are encoded by language and tradition. *Narration* is also Ricoeur's second step, after description, in his understanding of the moral self as an interpretive and dialogical self. Some narrative generally holds together and integrates the hierarchies of our encoded ethical practices. Some narrative gives the final meaning to our means-end actions, our if-then actions, our plans of life, and our images of the good life. To develop as a moral person, one must assimilate the classic narratives of one's tradition—those that over time have proved most capable of giving meaning to our ethical struggles and losses. In the words of Hans-Georg Gadamer, from whom Ricoeur has learned so much, development toward morality requires learning to interpret the "classics" of a tradition.[26] Ricoeur understands these classics to be primarily narrative classics, generally religious in scope.

But in spite of this emphasis on the role in ethics of inherited communal practices and traditions, Ricoeur goes beyond the traditionalism of most forms of communitarianism. Ethical action at this stage deals with only communally patterned goods and aspirations; we have not yet arrived at the arena of full morality. Why is it that our ethical aspirations toward the premoral goods of life do not, in themselves, deal with the core of genuine moral maturity for persons? The answer seems to be this: according to Ricoeur, the goods of life conflict and thereby produce various forms of strife or even violence.

As I indicated above, the field of ethics, in contrast to the arena of morality, is born out of our purposive search for the premoral good. This is an insight that much of modern psychotherapy, both secular and religious, unwittingly recognizes. Much of psychotherapy helps us identify and pursue the premoral goods of life. In this sense, the therapies deal with the ethical but not necessarily the fully moral. However, many forms of family, couple, and group psychotherapy, as we will see in chapter 6, actually do deal with both ethics and morality because they more directly address the full field of human conflict. Morality itself assumes and builds on our ethical and teleological aspirations, but it also goes beyond them.[27] This is why most individual psychotherapies that enable persons to better identify and pursue the goods of life are morally relevant even though not morally definitive. These therapies address the level of morality that Owen Flanagan called the PMPR level of morality (the Principle of Minimum Psychological Realism). He meant by this the premoral level of morality, often illuminated by the empirical sciences, which the more properly moral level always assumes but also further refines and reconciles. This is an insight that the modern therapies do not fully understand when some inflate their views of the premoral good of health prematurely into models of maturity and morality, as some of their critics in the 1970s and 1980s properly observed. Morality in the full sense of the word is born out of the tragic conflict between the goods of life.

Morality, in contrast to ethics, mediates conflicts between premoral goods and the persons seeking these goods.[28] It does this by employing tests determining which of our moral maxims are universalizable. One such test can be found in Kant's second formulation of the categorical imperative, which says, "Act so that you treat humanity, whether in your own person or in that of another, always as an end and never as a means only."[29] In the context of religions such as Judaism and Christianity, and other religions as well, one finds similar tests in various formulations of the Golden Rule. In Christianity, we also find the principle of neighbor love: "You shall love your neighbor as yourself" (Matt. 22:39). These principles show solicitude and respect for both other and self, tell us to treat all persons as ends and never as means alone, and generally imply that we should recognize that in their humanity alone *all* individuals are deserving of just access to the premoral goods of life.[30] Actions pursuing goods that pass this test of universalization are moral actions in contrast to simply worthy ethical aspirations. The popular psychotherapies that I analyzed in the 1970s and 1980s too frequently projected cultural images of human fulfillment based, in Ricoeur's terms, on the field of ethics but often failed to distinguish these images from the fully moral.

It is at the moment of this test—what Ricoeur called the "deontological test"—that Kohlberg's Kantian-like model of moral thinking would be valued and would find a place within Ricoeur's more multidimensional hermeneutic theory of moral thought and action. As revealed above, Kohlberg's thin view of moral thinking finds little place for ethics as the pursuit of the goods of life. Furthermore, it finds no place for tradition and the narrative classics that give broader meaning to our ethical strivings. But because Ricoeur can include Kantian and Kohlbergian critical tests within his more encompassing teleological and tradition-based narrative approach, he can also criticize all positions in philosophy (Alasdair MacIntyre), moral theology (Stanley Hauerwas), or psychology (Paul Vitz) that reduce morality to the virtues and narratives of a tradition.[31] The practices of traditions, in his view, can be, and must be at times, critiqued.

In discussing the test of universalization, Ricoeur already has moved into the third aspect of the dialogical self as moral agent: the moment of *prescription*. But prescription for Ricoeur has several dimensions to it. First, Ricoeur has given us a synthesis of two great—and often thought to be conflicting—models of philosophical ethics. He has brought together Aristotle and Kant by disciplining Aristotle's ethics of desire, habit, virtue, and community formation with the tests of Kant's morality of the categorical imperative and other similar principles of universalization, such as the Golden Rule and the principle of neighbor love.

But for Ricoeur, this test is still not enough to provide a full statement of the nature of moral reflection and action. There must be, according to him, a moment of wisdom where the moral actor returns to the original concrete situation of action. The tests of our ethical strivings for the premoral goods of life found in the universalization principle of the categorical imperative, the Golden Rule, or the love commandment should now be fine-tuned to the actual constraints of specific situations and the concrete goods that are there at stake. Ordering and ranking these conflicting goods requires a judgment of *phronêsis*—that is, a judgment of practical reason or practical wisdom. This is a matter of being wise. It requires taking seriously the situation in all of its complications and ambiguity. This is a turn to the *Sittlichkeit*; this is the point at which Ricoeur supplements Aristotle's teleology and Kant's deontology with the situationalism of Hegel. It is now, however, a situationalism guided by the narratives and virtues of a classic tradition and the tests of universalization, rather than some form of simple utilitarianism that generally guides situation ethics.[32]

Moral deliberation in Ricoeur's model is inextricably related to understanding and interpretation. Something like this model of moral reflection and action should guide our social, cultural, and religious effort to develop moral persons. Something like this model should guide our human and social sciences in their research to grasp the more detailed conditions for moral development. And something like the view of moral action should be available when assessing the end results of our psychotherapies.

As I have suggested, when Ricoeur makes the distinction between ethics and morality, he is paralleling Frankena's distinction between the nonmoral and the moral, or Janssens's distinction between the premoral and the moral. This distinction is making a very powerful point that Frankena's terminology hides but that, on the other hand, Janssens's terminology reveals. This is the idea that the moral is dependent on the premoral. Although the *ought* of the fully moral cannot be derived from the *is* of the premoral, the *ought* of the moral requires insight into the *is* of the premoral. In this view, there can be no radical separation of *ought* from *is*.

This insight into the importance of the premoral for the fully moral is driving the new rapprochement among the normative disciplines of moral philosophy, moral theology, and the contemporary moral psychologies. As Kwame Appiah has observed in his recent book *Experiments in Ethics* (2008), those advocating a radical separation between *is* and *ought*, whether they be like Kant or G. E. Moore, are out of fashion. And those understanding that the moral builds on, helps actualize, and yet resolves conflicts between our competing premoral goods are gaining central visibility today in the normative disciplines. This is why figures such as William James, who tried to bring the empirical and the normative disciplines together, are increasingly honored today. Appiah uses the word *evaluations* to describe our basic emotional responses—whether they be conceptualized as humanistic psychology's organismic actualization tendency, the adaptive retentions of evolutionary psychology, or the moral intuitions studied by Joshua Greene, Jonathan Haidt, and their colleagues.[33] We may be justified in calling these basic responses good in some premoral sense, but not if we call them fully moral. Appiah writes: "We cannot content ourselves with the claim that a given bundle of attitudes solves a social coordination problem—that it is, from some objective point of view, adaptive. That is a possible standard for a heuristic, but . . . it's not moral in nature."[34] Although judgments of evaluation and more fully moral judgments are distinguishable, they do not need to be dichotomized. Appiah concludes:

> Our moral world is both caused and created, and its breezes carry the voices of both explanations and reasons. In moving from the psychologist's concern with naturalistic explanation to the philosopher's concern with reasons, we move from the issue of what sort of dispositions it might be good for us to have to the issue of what sorts of sentiments might count as moral justifications.[35]

The Five Dimensions of Moral Reflection

Although Ricoeur makes the useful distinction between ethics and morality, and hence between the premoral and the moral, he makes other important distinctions as well that are important for the task of critique. In fact, Ricoeur's full theory of morality contains five dimensions, which I want to uncover and use to assess the images of fulfillment in both psychotherapy and spirituality. As we have seen, there is first of all the ethical or *teleological* dimension—the dimension that drives our strivings to realize fundamental premoral desires and human tendencies. Second, there is the dimension of *practices*—the habits and traditions that, in their more classic forms, reveal our more tested premoral goods and the most effective behaviors in realizing them. Third, there is the *narrative* dimension—the stories, often religious in scope, that give both meaning and some justification to our strivings. Fourth, there is the more distinctively moral or *deontological* dimension, which attempts to resolve conflicts among competing goods both within ourselves and between us and others. This deontological dimension or principle is generally embedded in a larger narrative, as the Golden Rule is embedded within the narrative of creation and redemption in both Judaism and Christianity. Finally, there is the *situational* or *contextual* dimension, in which we must make judgments in light of the constraints and pressures of specific contexts. Those familiar with my work in practical theology,[36] cultural critique,[37] and moral psychology[38] will recognize in this list my five dimensions of practical moral reason. Ricoeur is one of my sources for this framework.

The Five Dimensions and the Contemporary Science-Religion Discussion

I will now try to interrelate and make illustrative commentary on various perspectives in the science-religion discussion as they relate to the five dimensions of moral judgment and action. This discussion will be more illustrative than exhaustive. But I hope it will be suggestive for how science and religion—particularly the dialogue among psychology, spirituality, *and* the normative disciplines of philosophy and theology—can come together and provide a richer framework for assessing and critiquing psychotherapeutic and spiritual practices.

Most important to this discussion, as I have argued, is Ricoeur's insistence on the priority of ethics over morality, or, to say it in the language of Louis Janssens, the dependence of the moral on the premoral. With these distinctions in mind, we have new grounds for understanding the enormous contributions that the social sciences are making today to our understanding of human flourishing. Theologians, moral philosophers, and political philosophers complain because everywhere they look, society seems to be turning to the social sciences for guidance on issues in education, mental health, economic well-being, the nature of human happiness—in fact, any issue that addresses the broad question of what constitutes human flourishing. Although in the 1970s and 1980s I criticized much of the culture of the psychotherapies for making too much of the actualization tendency of humanistic psychology and its implied nonhedonic ethical egoism, Ricoeur's and Appiah's neo-Aristotelian emphasis on the priority of ethics and the neo-Thomist Janssen's emphasis on the priority of the premoral give me reason to fine-tune this criticism. Much of good psychotherapy rightly concentrates on restoring healthy emotionality and basic human capacities. It does this with the faith that, in turn, this will make the person at least a bit more loving, generous, and possibly even just. This hope—this rather inarticulate faith—is possibly based on something like the belief held by Ricoeur, Appiah, and Janssens that justice and fairness of the more properly moral kind feed on the teleological aspirations of the ethical and premoral. There is little doubt that in the hands of an Albert Ellis,[39] the more romantic lapses of Fritz Perls, Rogers, or Maslow,[40] or even the late Heinz Kohut's theory of motivation,[41] the impression could arise that they believed all authentic self-actualizations should rather easily harmonize with one another, both within the self and between the self and others. Much of this literature gave rise to an image of a world without conflict—a world somewhat like Adam Smith's view of the hidden hand of a capitalist society harmonizing the acquisitive feelings and actions of all individual parties. The actual practice of these various therapies was probably better than the cultural images of health and fulfillment projected in their written literature. But if the insight holds about the priority of the ethical and the premoral for the goals of the moral, my earlier critique would need to be moderated, if not in substance, at least in tone.

The Place of Evolutionary Psychology

The distinction between ethics and morality and between the premoral and the moral is, however, also useful for assessing the relevance to morality of evolutionary psychology and moral intuitionism. First, I turn to evolutionary psychology and its precursor sociobiology. E. O. Wilson on several occasions struggles to make this distinction between ethics and morality when developing his claims that human morality is grounded in biology. For example, in his book *On Human Nature* (1978), Wilson argues that traditional transcendent values and goals integrating society, mainly provided by religion, have collapsed one by one. Then he writes: "In order to search for a new morality based upon a more truthful definition of man, it is necessary to look inward, to dissect the machinery of the mind and to retrace its evolutionary history."[42] This is the kind of statement widely present in much of the literature of sociobiology and evolutionary psychology. It tends to hold that our values come not from tradition or religion and certainly not from any transcendent source but, rather, from our biology, and that, to gain a firmer grasp of what they actually are, we must look inward and dissect our evolutionary history or, as many neuroscientists would claim, dissect our brain. Philosophers will identify this as a foundationalist program that downplays the accomplishments of culture and tradition, that implicitly tells us to forget these sources of morality and rebuild our cultural values anew and from the ground up on the basis of a better understanding of our biology. Ricoeur and Appiah, who both respect biology's possible contribution, would say this goes too far. It ends in virtually alienating us from the accomplishments—indeed the classics—of our cultural traditions.

It is interesting to note that Wilson himself soon follows this statement with another that recognizes the limitations of biology. His foundationalist agenda of turning inward to biology and the brain will give rise to another dilemma. Wilson writes: "But that effort, I predict, will uncover the second dilemma, which is the choice that must be made among the ethical premises inherent in man's biological nature."[43] He goes on to say that "innate censors and motivations exist in the brain that deeply and unconsciously affect our ethical premises; from these roots, morality evolved as instinct."[44] In Wilson's view, the new dilemma that science will bring us is this: "Which of the censors and motivators should be obeyed and which ones might better be curtailed or sublimated?"[45]

Here he acknowledges the conflicting premoral values of our own biology—conflicts that lead us to the threshold of what Ricoeur calls morality. Here he has in mind the biological roots of our empathy, investment in our children, respect for authority, and reciprocity toward kin and neighbors as contributors to morality. But he also has in mind the biological grounds of our egoism, aggression, nepotism, and what today's moral psychologists call our biological tendency to see the fault in others before we recognize it in ourselves.[46] Wilson realizes that we have to choose between our conflicting biological tendencies.

The sad thing is that Wilson, as do many of his followers, seems to think that biology alone can resolve this conflict. Ricoeur would say that biology can make its contribution but that we finally must resort to the classic practices of a cultural tradition, to a deepened understanding of a culture's founding narratives, something like the deontological critique of the Golden Rule, and to refined understandings of the selective pressures of various situations and contexts in order to handle the challenges of Wilson's new dilemma. In conclusion, evolutionary psychology and sociobiology can contribute to ethics, but their contribution to morality must be mediated by a much more complex interpretive process.

The Place of the New Moral Intuitionism

Ricoeur does not address the new moral intuitionism in moral psychology. But Appiah does and, without relying on Ricoeur, his response to its claims are similar to what Ricoeur might say. Appiah gives a great deal of attention to the claims of Jonathan Haidt and his colleagues that humans have inherited a number of "learning modules" that lead them to respond to moral issues with intuitive prereflective "flashes" of mental response.[47] Haidt believes that our moral lives are primarily driven by what he calls these "moral emotions," which are built around various neural systems of the brain and are there because at some time in our evolutionary history they gave us rapid-fire adaptive responses that enabled us to handle threats from our environment.[48] He acknowledges that not all of these so-called moral emotions are equally relevant to the moral demands of modern civilizations and that some seem directly at odds with the liberal political philosophies of most Western democracies.[49] Furthermore, they are so powerful, so automatic and instinctual, that once our moral thinking is tilted in the direction of these innate and primitive moral emotions, our second-order moral deliberations are often no more than "confabulations" or rationalizations of positive and negative emotions functioning at more primitive and intuitive levels.[50]

In contrast to much of humanistic psychology, which sees the human self as more or less naturally unified around a central actualization tendency, Haidt sees it as a series of conflicting modules—for example, between what he likes to metaphorically call the elephant (our instinctual life) and the rider (our deliberative life), between the left-hemisphere storytelling and interpretive brain and the right-hemisphere analytic brain, the old brain (consisting of spinal nerves, midbrain, and forebrain) and the new brain (consisting of neocortex and orbital frontal cortex).[51] The conflicting nature of our premoral ethical strivings are, for Haidt, a given of human nature.

Haidt believes he has identified several basic moral emotions, intuitions, or learning modules. His most recent list seems to include emotions of avoidance, hierarchy and respect, purity and pollution, fairness and reciprocity, in-group and out-group, and awe and elevation.[52] Haidt claims he has achieved insight into these moral emotions and intuitions by telling research subjects stories and then recording their responses. In one article, he writes: "In my dissertation and my other early studies, I told people short stories in which a person does something disgusting or disrespectful that was perfectly harmless (for example, a family cooks and eats its dog, after the dog was killed by a car). I was trying to pit the emotion of disgust against reasoning about harm and individual rights."[53]

He found that disgust won out in all the groups that he studied in Brazil, India, and the United States with the exception of students in liberal colleges and universities who tended to say that people have the right to do whatever they want as long as it does not harm anyone. Haidt concludes that emotion played a bigger role in moral judgment than cognitive developmental theorists like Kohlberg have tended to believe. Haidt's work on the so-called moral emotions is full of such illustrations.

Along with the work of Joshua Greene, Martin Seligman, and many others, Haidt is initiating a new direction in moral and positive psychology. But his work seems to beg for something like the distinction between ethics and morality and between premoral and moral goods that I have been developing in this chapter. Why does Haidt call these automatic responses moral intuitions or emotions? Does he believe that they are indeed always fully moral? No, he does not. Does he believe that sometime in human evolutionary history they may have been adaptive, maybe have even contributed to human flourishing in some time and place? Yes, he does. But doesn't this mean that such emotions should be seen as premoral rather than fully moral? I believe that would be a more satisfying language for the real meaning of his contributions. Kwame Appiah tends to agree when he, in his discussion of Haidt, does grant these emotions the status of "evaluations" but not full moral judgments.

Appiah does not believe he is undermining the existence of second-order deliberative judgments when he acknowledges the existence, and perhaps heuristic usefulness, of first-order intuitive emotions of a premoral kind. Haidt, as we noticed above, almost dismantles second-order deliberations, whether they be something like Kant's categorical imperative, Ricoeur's deontological test, or the ultilitarian maximizations of the overall good.

Haidt is much more like philosopher David Hume in seeing reason as being in the service of the passions or the rider in the service of the elephant, to use Haidt's preferred metaphors for the human mind.

But in a few places Haidt rather weakly admits that there may be a place for something like Kant's, Kohlberg's, or Ricoeur's deontological test. He writes: "I do agree with Josh Greene that sometimes we can use controlled processes such as reasoning to override our initial intuitions. I just think this happens rarely, maybe in one or two percent of the hundreds of judgments we make each week."[54] It is clear that, being the political liberal that he confesses to be, Haidt must finally acknowledge the possibility of moving from the premoral to a more fully moral point of view, thereby coordinating and sometimes subordinating our deep intuitions. Unfortunately, however, his research, to my knowledge, has given us little insight into the conditions that can bring about more adequate second-order deliberations.

Classic Practices and the Deontological Test

Space limitations require me to address the remaining three dimensions of practical moral thinking more in the form of brief notations that I will expand later in this book. So far, I have been developing the first dimension—the idea that morality builds on our premoral desires for the good life. Earlier, I stated that we cannot know adequately even the goods of life by directly consulting our biological inclinations, as important as they are. I concurred with Gadamer, Ricoeur, and MacIntyre that our inherited cultural practices have learned much about the reliable goods of life and even more about how to pursue them. Rogers used to encourage his clients to trust their organismic experiencing, but I wager that careful analyses of verbal exchanges between therapist and client would demonstrate that his client's feelings were often encoded by linguistic cultural practices, some of which his therapy helped the client to trust, reject, or revise on broad interpretive grounds that included but went beyond the client's raw feelings.

Some of these interpretive grounds, I wager, were implicit deontological tests that the therapeutic exchange itself enabled the client to examine. Clients themselves sometimes ask, and rightly, Is this fair? Is this just? And what if everyone did what I feel like doing? Does moral psychology today have much to teach us about the relation of such tests as the categorical imperative, the Golden Rule, or the principle of neighbor love to our actual psychological life? I think that it does, but even then its contributions need evaluation from philosophy and theology. In recent writings, both Haidt and cognitive neuroscientist Donald Pfaff have criticized these classic principles and moral tests. Haidt argues that such principles are stated far too abstractly and are far too divorced from the totality of our affective lives and needs for attachment.[55] And insofar as the deontological test stands alone, as it does in Kant and Hobbes, and is disconnected from our affective life, Haidt and Pfaff are right. But if we follow Ricoeur and Appiah on the role of the affections in morality, Haidt's criticisms have less force.

But the research of Don Pfaff in his provocative book *The Neuroscience of Fair Play: Why We (Usually) Follow the Golden Rule* (2007) advances an explanation that completely anchors these principles in the neural systems of our brains, even to the place that eliminates the role of both the teachings of tradition and the deliberations of rationality.[56] Pfaff claims that our capacity to follow the Golden Rule springs entirely from two overlapping emotional systems of our brains. One system has to do with our capacity to detect fear, anxiety, and danger and is primarily located in the amygdala. The other system has to do with sex and parenting and is stimulated by estrogen in women or by the flow of testosterone in men and is moved by our genetic drive toward inclusive fitness.

According to Pfaff, both systems give rise to the Golden Rule by blurring the distinction between self and other. In the case of the negative fear-pain system, we feel the other's pain as if it were our own.[57] A similar blurring of the distinction between self and other happens in the positive sex and parenting system. Pfaff believes that this blurring occurs primarily through the mirroring of emotional excitation—something close to what Spazio meant by the idea of simulation. And, in an effort to be scientific in the most theoretically economic way possible, he believes that this blurring of self and other happens without the mediation of ideals about equality or any actual concrete teaching such as the Golden Rule, the principle of neighbor love, or Kant's categorical imperative. It occurs because, under the conditions of emotional excitation, there is a loss of information about the separateness of self and other. Here are Pfaff's own words:

> From a scientific point of view, the simple explanations of any phenomena, even complex phenomena, are best. The explanation I propose is very simple in the sense that it does not suppose all kinds of special superhuman capacities for people to act altruistically or avoid hurting each other—no fancy nervous contraptions, no big deal. It does not even require the individual to learn anything in order to behave in an ethical fashion. I simply posit a *loss of information*. That is an opaque neuroscientific expression, but a basic one, and so wonderfully easy to explain that a person with ordinary common sense, or even a neuroscientist, can easily believe it.[58]

I appreciate Pfaff's strong introduction of the emotional life into our understanding of what Ricoeur has called the deontological test. It shows that respecting the other means identifying empathically with the emotional life of the other—the possible negative harms and possible life-giving affections. But on several grounds, I also resist it as an overstatement.

First, I resist it because Pfaff seems to assume he is discovering something about the role of affections in the Golden Rule that was overlooked by the ancients. Those of you who know Rabbi Hillel's formulation of the Golden Rule will know that he introduces a role for the emotions. Ricoeur has noticed this and has used Hillel's formulation as a justification for closely relating the deontological test to the priority of ethics as emotional striving toward the goods of life. Don't we hear anticipations of Pfaff on the role of negative and positive emotions in the Golden Rule when Ricoeur writes, "I read in Hillel 'do not do to your fellow what you hate to have done to you'"? Then he sees a formulation that shifts from the emotionally negative position of hate and harm to something more emotionally positive when Ricoeur says, "We read a similar formulation in Matthew, in the Sermon on the Mount (7:12), 'So whatever you wish that men would do to you, do so to them. . . .' Although one of these obligations is negative and the other positive, they are in fact equivalent."[59]

Second, I find it strange that Pfaff thinks he must renounce the role of ideas, ideals, and narratives in fostering what he is calling the Golden Rule. In both Judaism and Christianity, we are taught that we should treat the other as ourselves because both self and other are children of God and made in God's image. Therefore, the status of both self and other before God is viewed as the basis for both self-respect and other-regard. This ontological claim about the status of humans is ensconced in a biblical narrative about a good Creator God creating a good world. Pfaff may be partially correct in arguing that negative and positive emotional contagion blurs the distinction between self and other and gives rise to empathy toward the other.

But does it have to be one way or the other? Do we have to choose between emotions and ideas? Might a more fruitful research agenda be one that attempts to gain insight into how the classic teachings about the Golden Rule, carried by powerful religious and other institutions throughout history, interact with our various emotional neural networks to create long-lasting and enduring habits of empathy and mutual identification? Why rule out the narrative level of mental life altogether? As sympathetic as Kwame Appiah is to experimentalism in moral philosophy, he warns against allowing that interest to deprive us of insights into the role of narratives and stories in our moral life. He writes: "We wouldn't recognize a community as human if it had no stories, if its people had no narrative imagination. From the standpoint of *Verstandeswelt,* we recognize exchanging stories as one of the things humanly worth doing."[60]

I will delay discussing Ricoeur's last dimension—the turn to context and situation—until the next chapter. I also will delay to a later chapter a fuller employment of this moral framework for evaluating the images of change in some examples of spirituality. I hope that so far I have at least outlined a position—building on moral psychology, philosophy, and theology—that will help us become oriented to the task of critique in both psychotherapy and spirituality, one that would complicate and nuance some of my earlier efforts.

4

Religion, Science,
and the New Spirituality

What has the dialogue between science and religion contributed to the recent cultural interest in spirituality? And what has the scientific study of spirituality contributed to our understanding of how to define it?

Whatever the science-religion conversation has contributed to our view of spirituality, it has not exercised its influence in a vacuum. The scientific interest in this phenomenon interacts with a variety of other cultural and social trends. Its influence is blended with these other forces, contexts, and situations. I will elaborate on this point in a moment. First, however, I will advance a thesis. The scientific study of spiritual transformation has tended to give us a much more inner-worldly view of spirituality. This new spirituality tends to be built around the importance of human connections (family, loved ones, and friendships), work or vocation, and practical judgments or practical reason that supports human flourishing. There is a transcendent dimension to this spirituality, but it is one that both reinforces yet sometimes relativizes these more earthly goods.

This new spirituality, however, may be undermining the remainder of a more two-tiered view of spirituality, a view perhaps best exemplified by but not limited to medieval Roman Catholicism. This older view distinguished between a higher, other-worldly clerical spirituality and a this-worldly spirituality of the laity.[1] It might be argued that science has interacted with a more distinctively Protestant view that challenged the distinction between lay and clerical spirituality and saw spirituality more in terms of various vocations in this life.[2] One can see evidence of this new spirituality in the emphasis on eudaemonism or human flourishing in the science, religion, and spirituality writings of Owen Flanagan, the positive psychology of Jonathan Haidt, the work on character by Martin Seligman and Chris Peterson, and the research on the connection of sociality, health, and spirituality in the work on loneliness by John Cacioppo.[3]

This new emphasis on the importance of human connections in family and friendships as well as work and vocation can also be seen in the commentary on new directions of Roman Catholic spirituality put forward by Boston University scholar Claire Wolfteich. Much of recent Catholic spirituality has featured the needs of laypeople—laypeople who live, love, and work in a practical world that encompasses both private and public spaces. Wolfteich writes:

> Imbedded in debates about the meaning of politics, work, and family are deep spiritual questions. Work and family are primary spheres of lay action and responsibility, hence logical loci for spirituality. People often define themselves through their work and their family relationships, which become centers of meaning or alienation.[4]

Wolfteich sees another preoccupation of contemporary spirituality: a concern about the nature of practical reason. For laypeople to make judgments about the nature of their relationships and their work life, they must exercise practical wisdom. If their spirituality is to help them, Wolfteich believes it must also inform their practical reason in making decisions in both their private and public worlds. She writes:

If the religious person is to engage faith with work in the public sphere, then he or she must be guided in discernment. . . . Laity must make choices in their private relationships, at work, and in public responsibilities. If they are to be "leaven in the world," then they must daily make practical judgments consistent with this mission. It is important, then, to think through the relationship between faith and practical reason.[5]

It is my view that the science-religion dialogue and the social trends influencing contemporary spirituality are giving rise to a revived religious humanism in which transcendence and tradition are being searched for their relevance to the challenges of human relationships, work life, and the practical reason needed to guide these concerns.

In addition to the influence of science on forms of present-day spirituality, the forces of modernization and secularization have exhibited strong pressure to give spirituality a more inner-worldly cast. Modernization, as sociologists and economists tell us, differentiates the social structures of society and introduces into the lives of us all multiple logics and patterns that are not easily accommodated by any particular inherited ethic, be it religious or secular. Laypeople live very complicated lives with many different demands from their economic, domestic, and political spheres of daily activity. It should not be surprising that they increasingly search for spiritualities that help them cope with these diverse demands. The situation and context of modernization itself, to which the Protestant Reformation was doubtless an early responder, has influenced our spirituality to become more this-worldly and practical.

Note that I have mentioned the words *situation* and *context*. I introduced these words in chapter 3 in connection with Paul Ricoeur's list of several steps of practical moral reflection and action. According to Ricoeur, not only is ethics born out of our teleological strivings for the goods of life, morally critiqued by what he calls the deontological test, and enriched by inherited classic practices and narratives, but our moral thinking should return to and address the original situation of our concrete ethical conflicts. The move from ethics to morality must be completed by a return to the situation—the *Sittlichkeit*.

But the words *situation* and *context* open complex issues in contemporary discussions about morality and practical reason. Some social psychologists like to flash evidence before philosophers and theologians that suggest that nothing as sophisticated as Ricoeur's model actually guides our decisions in the real world. These psychologists claim that the pressures of the situation dictate our responses more than we like to think. They insist that neither global character traits nor reliable moral deliberation truly guides humans when confronting the immediacy of moral and practical conflicts. Rather, as Kwame Appiah summarizes their argument, many social psychologists believe people are more likely to be guided "by systematic human tendencies to respond to features of their situations."[6] And, indeed, does this mean that to recognize the pressures of modernity on our images of spirituality, as I did above, might itself be an example of this kind of situational pressure?

I believe that there is a limited truth to this emphasis by some social psychologists on the influence of situations on moral and practical decisions. But it can be overstated. Yes, under the pressure of social forces requiring rapid decisions, the power of situations is doubtless very significant. But many of our moral decisions or moral directions are more gradually arrived at in response to a series of situations or on the basis of a synthesis of more specific situations. This is why, as Appiah wisely points out, human beings rely so heavily on institutions. Institutions habituate and reinforce traditions of good decisions and make it possible for us to resist the pressures of immediate situations.

Appiah's point is close to Ricoeur's view about how our inherited classic practices provide guides to both the tested good and the right. Appiah says it well when he agrees with philosopher Gil Harman "that if we want to improve human welfare, we may do better to 'put less emphasis on moral education and on building character and more emphasis on trying to arrange social institutions so that human beings are not placed in situations in which they will act badly.'"[7] It will be my argument that the new science of spiritual transformation plus the collective experiences of modernization can and should intentionally join with inherited traditions to give institutional form to a more inner-worldly spirituality—a spirituality I have called a *revived religious humanism*.

One might think my claim that science has contributed to this inner-worldly spirituality—especially its possible institutionalization into a revived religious humanism—is something of a stretch. It could be easier, however, to think that just the opposite is true. Robert Fuller's engaging book *Spiritual but Not Religious* (2001) summarizes a great deal of the current perception of the rise of spirituality in its more individualistic forms and the decline of institutional religion.[8] Much of the scientific study of spirituality mainly has to do with its effects on health and often uses such thin measures of spirituality as frequency of prayer, church membership or attendance, or belief in God to do its work.[9] Such interests and measures themselves cast science as something of a wedge disconnecting spirituality from its larger liturgical, moral, communal, and institutional settings. Research by neuroscientists such as Andrew Newberg has shown neural effects of meditation and of alleged experiences of the transcendent but seldom demonstrates interest in the full effects of the communal, liturgical, and religious way of life.[10] In view of these trends, one might think that the evidence contradicts my thesis and that science is undermining an institutional form of spiritual life, whether completely humanistic or recognizably theistic.

But there are other ways to look at this evidence. The facts showing that hospitals and medical schools are now interested in the health consequences of spirituality, that there is a new worldwide movement in positive psychology and other disciplines that are comparing spiritualities, and that religious institutions of all kinds even today often take account of this new information as they explain the value of their own ethics, doctrines, and liturgies[11] indicate to me that the scientific study of spiritual transformation is influencing institutional life, both religious and secular, and in this way is therefore supporting a revived religious humanism with institutional form.

Examples of the New Spirituality

Examples of the way science is feeding this more inner-worldly spirituality are not difficult to find. I turn first to Jonathan Haidt, a leading figure in the new positive psychology.

Haidt on Attachment, Family, and Work

As we already have observed, Haidt, along with Chris Peterson and Martin Seligman, intentionally promotes a dialogue between the world's traditions of spiritual wisdom and modern psychology. Haidt does not believe that modern psychology originates by itself insights into what makes humans happy and flourishing. He claims that many of the present themes of positive psychology can be found in the great wisdom traditions of China, India, and the Mediterranean.[12] It is quite clear, however, that Haidt feels positive psychology can sometimes refine these spiritualities and, in some cases, actually correct them, as he tries to do with aspects of Stoic, Buddhist, and Christian spirituality. Implicitly, Haidt practices something like Ricoeur's dialectic of understanding-explanation-understanding, which I advocated in chapter 1. But, as does much of positive psychology, he often short-circuits historical understanding and uses psychological explanations to make controversial normative judgments——sometimes, I might add, with a degree of acuity.

Haidt is interested in the category of happiness when discussing the spiritual ends of humans. Not all spiritualities, however, gravitate to the goal of happiness. Protestant spirituality is more interested in salvation and justification than in happiness as such. On the other hand, Roman Catholic spirituality synthesized the rubrics of Christian salvation and Greek happiness in its belief that the rational love of God was the fulfillment of both happiness and salvation.[13] Be aware that in my defense in chapter 2 of the caritas view of love, in contrast to the strong agape or eros models, I was sympathetic with the Roman Catholic synthesis of happiness and salvation. With this caveat in mind, I turn to examine how Haidt's science might influence spirituality in an inner-worldly direction.

Haidt believes that happiness is associated with a rich life of human attachments and meaningful work. Hence, both similar to but in ways far different from Freud, love and work are the two values that Haidt believes lead to flourishing and happiness. Early in his book *The Happiness Hypothesis,* he sets forth a formula for happiness: H (happiness) = S (our inherited temperament set point) plus C (conditions) plus V (voluntary activities).[14] Haidt characterizes love and work as mainly external conditions. He writes: "Love and work are, for people, obvious analogues to water and sunshine for plants."[15] Haidt believes that the West has typically emphasized the external conditions needed for flourishing and that the East, especially Buddhism, more generally has accentuated internal voluntary attitudes and states of mind.

Haidt thinks that both external conditions and internal attitudes are necessary for a healthy spirituality. He is, however, frankly critical of the spirituality of Buddhism for making too much of internal voluntary attitudes, such as control of desire. But he is equally critical of the spirituality of Western agapic love, which he believes sees love as abstract and does not fully understand the deep roles of human affections and attachments. In his criticism of both East and West, we can see that Haidt, like many figures in positive psychology, thinks the spiritual traditions of the world contain wisdom—a wisdom, however, that desperately needs not only the refinements of modern science but the explanations and corrections of science as well.

I will argue that Haidt and his positive psychology colleagues may be right that science can contribute refinements to a spiritual tradition. But they often overstate their recommended refinements to the place that they become actual corrections of a spiritual tradition by science—corrections that place science above tradition and that are not fully informed. This happens because they do not commit sufficient effort to achieving a full hermeneutical and historically nuanced understanding and retrieval of these complex traditions.

Haidt has less to say about the importance of work for human flourishing than he does about attachments and love. On this topic, however, he does discuss the observations of the great animal researcher Harry Harlowe. Harlowe noticed that apes and monkeys seemed to enjoy playing, solving problems, and causing things to happen "just for the fun of it." They did these things without the imagined rewards or reinforcements that behaviorism posited. And Haidt discusses the elegant theoretical work of Harvard psychologist Robert White, who argued that both psychoanalysis and behaviorism overlooked that

> . . . people and many other mammals have a basic drive to make things happen. You can see it in the joy infants take with "busy boxes," the activity centers that allow them to convert flailing arm movements into ringing bells and spinning wheels. . . . Psychologists have referred to this basic need as a need for competence, industry, or mastery. White called it the "effectance motive," which he defined as the need or drive to develop competence through interacting with and controlling one's environment.[16]

Haidt mentions research showing that a sense of effectance is enhanced if one's work permits a degree of "occupational self-direction."[17] And he acknowledges that one's work will be all the more meaningful if it is guided by a sense of calling or vocation. But he has little to say about what the great concept of vocation or calling, more thoroughly elaborated by the theologians of the Protestant Reformation, really means and adds to the psychobiological need for effectance.

Haidt has much more to say about the other values he uses to judge world spiritualities, that is, the values of human attachments, connections, and love. Haidt turns to the work of John Bowlby and his collaborator Mary Ainsworth, which shows how important early attachments between mother and child are for later relationship formation, health, happiness, well-being, and even spirituality.[18] Haidt agrees with the views espoused by John Cacioppo and William Patrick in their recent book *Loneliness: Human Nature and the Need for Social Connection* (2008).[19] According to Haidt, people who have fewer social bonds and undergo the pain of loneliness also have poorer health, higher rates of suicide, more cognitive impairment, more alcoholism, and less reported satisfaction with life.[20] Similarly, Haidt believes that "having strong social relationships strengthens the immune system, extends life (more than does quitting smoking), speeds recovery from surgery, and reduces the risks of depression and anxiety disorders."[21] He holds that the sociality played out in some spiritual communities enhances these human connections and their health-enhancing consequences.

Haidt joins Bowlby in asserting that good childhood attachments between parents and children set young persons on the road to better adult relationships, even a better chance for a healthy marriage. Haidt points out that in most mammals, there is little or no connection between parent-infant attachments and adult attachments between mates. For the most part, male mammals inseminate and then leave the child care to the mother. This is not so for human males, however, at least up to the present age. Both human males and females typically repeat their childhood attachments to parents with their mates and form lasting bonds to care for their offspring, creating the institution of marriage or at least some analogue to it. This bonding between male and female at the human level is, according to Haidt, due to two quirks of evolution for *Homo sapiens*: the big brains and large heads of human infants and the narrow pelvis of the human female, which also allows her ability to walk upright. This means that to be born at all, human infants must emerge early, when they are helpless and totally dependent for many months to come.

Haidt—along with many other anthropologists, evolutionary psychologists, and social neuroscientists—believes these facts of human evolution account for why human mothers need help raising their infants, why human males work out their "inclusive fitness" by investing in the long-term survival of their offspring, and why human males continue sexual consortium with their offsprings' mothers and collaborate with them in raising their mutual children. Haidt says that this accounts for why "a universal feature of human cultures is that men and women form relationships intended to last for years (marriage) that constrain their sexual behavior and in some way institutionalize their long-term ties to children and to each other."[22] If this seems like a familiar idea to you, I remind you that you heard something very similar to this in chapter 2 when I quoted the thirteenth-century Roman Catholic Thomas Aquinas. You will recall that he wrote the following:

> Yet nature does not incline thereto in the same way in all animals; since there are animals whose offspring are able to seek food immediately after birth, or are sufficiently fed by their mother; and in these there is no tie between male and female; whereas in those whose offspring needing the support of both parents, although for a short time, there is a certain tie, as may be seen in certain birds. In man, however, since the child needs the parents' care for a long time, there is a very great tie between male and female, to which tie even the generic nature inclines.[23]

But, as we will soon see, Haidt overlooks this strand of Christian thinking and what it means for recognizing the role of attachments in human and even Christian expressions of love and spirituality.

Of course, attachments can become conflicted and not always lead to happiness and well-being. Unhealthy ones can become a cause of anxiety, depression, and obsessive efforts to master them. Haidt recommends the kind of spirituality found in Buddhist meditation, or the cognitive therapy of Aaron Beck, or Prozac to gain release from destructive attachments.

Buddhists do this through mindful concentration on their own breathing or on some specific object. Beck does this with techniques for breaking destructive thought patterns such as personalization, overgeneralization, and magnification. Prozac accomplishes this through chemical effects that can liberate us from dysfunctional attachments and free us for more flexible and satisfying ones.[24]

Acknowledging this does not obscure the deeper truth that, according to Haidt and a growing consensus of researchers, relationships—generally first mediated by family and then radiated outward to larger society—get to the core of both happiness and spiritual well-being. This leads him, on the one hand, to recommend Buddhist meditation as a way of breaking troublesome and compulsive attachments while, on the other hand, to criticize both Stoicism and Buddhism for their overall philosophy of renunciation, which includes the eventual detachment from relationships as well. He writes:

> The life of cerebral reflection and emotional indifference (*apatheia*) advocated by many Greek and Roman philosophers and that of calm nonstriving advocated by Buddha are lives designed to avoid passion, and a life without passion is not a human life. Yes, attachments bring pain, but they also bring our greatest joys, and here is value in the very variation that the philosophers are trying to avoid.[25]

I detail Haidt's view of Stoic and Buddhist spirituality not to say he is correct in his assessment of them but to give an example of how he believes science can not only refine the spiritualities of the past but in some cases correct some of their deficiencies.

Haidt does much the same with Christian spiritualities. In his discussion of Christian love, Haidt neglects love as caritas and eros and seems to believe that Christian love was always and everywhere interpreted in terms of what I in chapter 2 called strong, self-sacrificial agape. In his commentary on Jesus' command that "you should love your neighbor as yourself" (Matt. 22:39), he writes:

> But what can it mean to love others as one loves oneself? The psychological origins of love are in attachment to parents and sexual partners. . . . *Agape* is a Greek word that refers to a kind of selfless, spiritual love with no sexuality, no clinging to a particular other person. . . . As in Plato, Christian love is stripped of its essential particularity, its focus on a specific other person. Love is remodeled into a general attitude toward a much larger, even infinite, class of objects.[26]

As we saw in that earlier discussion, sometimes Christian love was defined in these more abstract terms that gave no recognition to the origins of love in eros, that is, emotion and the close attachments with parents, siblings, and extended family. But that was not the case with Thomas Aquinas and the tradition he influenced. He gave a strong role to kin altruism in the origins of love and envisioned its generalization beyond family and kin by virtue of the Christian's recognition that all humankind are kin in the sense of being children of the divine parent God.

We also saw this in chapter 3 in Ricoeur's appreciation for the formulation of the Golden Rule given by Rabbi Hillel. Ricoeur wrote: "I read in Hillel 'do not do to your fellow what you hate to have done to you.'" The phrase "what you hate to have done to you" refers to the emotion of pain. This negative formulation points to the reality that the Jewish and Christian background to the principle of neighbor love was often fully aware of its emotional substructure in the positive experience of attachments and the negative deprivations of isolation, loneliness, and pain. Nor is Haidt aware of the very bodily formulations of neighbor love and the Golden Rule, such as the injunction in Ephesians that says:

In the same way, husbands should love their wives as they do their own bodies. He who loves his wife loves himself. For no one ever hates his own body, but he nourishes and tenderly cares for it, just as Christ does for the church, because we are members of his body (5:28-30).

Haidt approvingly acknowledges at one point that Christianity endorses the love of a man and a woman with marriage. But then he quickly adds: "But even this love is idealized as the love of Christ for his Church (Eph. 5:25)." This may be idealized, but it is not abstract and without emotion; within a very few verses, when Ephesians grounds marriage in Christ's enduring relationship to the church, we hear the very bodily metaphor commanding husbands to love their wives as their own bodies and to do this in analogy to Christ's bodily union with the church. Analogies of the body pervade Christian understandings of love as they pervade Christian understandings of community. Maybe Christian love was not always as abstract and idealized as Haidt thinks.

My purpose, however, is not to defend Christianity in this particular exchange between science and religion. My aim is to make a larger methodological point that I introduced in chapter 1. There I made the argument for the priority of the hermeneutical moment in the science-religion dialogue. This conversation will be most successful when the religious traditions that have shaped our effective histories are first of all understood and interpreted with care. When this happens, these traditions will be seen as complex conversations or dialogues with many different accents and tensions. More times than not, science will help refine opposing positions *within* a spiritual tradition rather than correcting or even dismantling the tradition as such. Although Haidt, and much of positive psychology, never explicitly set out to blatantly correct, dismantle, or belittle ancient spiritual traditions, in his strong emphasis on the value of relationships and work for healthy spirituality, Haidt ends up advancing correctives to both Christianity and Buddhism. In the case of Christianity, because I know it better, I think I successfully can argue that he did not so much correct the abstractness and idealism of its view of love as help emphasize one branch of interpretation in contrast to another within the same tradition.

One might be able to present a similar argument about Haidt's interpretation of Buddhism, that is, not so much that the Buddha was wrong but that interpreting this tradition's full conversation about the role of relationships in human flourishing is complex. We should be reminded that Buddhism, as does Hinduism, articulates a strong place for the role of the householder stage of life—the role of responsible parenthood, care of one's offspring, and maintenance of their provisions. In addition, the Buddhist scholar Alan Cole has argued that the true attitude of Buddhism toward relationships, especially family relationships, must be assessed in light of the doctrine of *samsara*, the wheel of rebirth. Here even the monk has his mind on his family, because being a monk earns merit for his mother, father, and siblings and enables their move as an entire family unit up the ladder of cosmic rebirth and eventual peace. And when family members support their son in the monastery or as a wandering monk with gifts and offerings, they are gaining merit and contributing to both his and their ascension in the cycle of rebirth. This is how, according to Cole, the family affections and ideology of Buddhism were both visible and regulated by what he calls the "patron-priest" relationship. Hence, the renunciation of attachments in Buddhism was more subtle than one might think. In the context of the full meaning of Buddhist life, what appeared to be renunciations were also indirect enhancements of family attachments at a higher and more cosmic level.[27]

In his chapter in *Children and Childhood in World Religions* (2009), Cole advances even more insight into how the more juicy aspects of human emotions serve as central symbols in various manifestations of Buddhism. Cole claims that "one stock rhetorical figure for explaining the Buddha's love for sentient beings is a comparison of the Buddha to a mother who has only one son." Cole writes:

Here as so often happens in religion, the private realm of family emotions is being deployed to construct its opposite: the world of invisible public religion, peopled by nonfamily members and their institutional representatives. Thus, with the Buddhas depicted as a kind of super-mother, one is made to understand that at least some of one's love for real family members should be redirected toward the Buddha in order to reciprocate the mother-love that he has been directing to each of us.[28]

Cole helps us see, in ways that Haidt overlooks, the prominence of emotions, attachments, and affections in this religion, which often is too easily classified as renouncing if not suppressing these dimensions of human life.

So, I conclude this discussion by reaffirming that science can help refine and balance traditions. In the case of spirituality, it can and has tended to render our inherited spiritualities more attentive to the inner-worldly values of relationships and work. To the extent that science has done this, it is and can contribute to a revived religious humanism. But this contribution will be most successful if made within an equally careful attempt to understand the complexity and fullness of these traditions. Scientific understanding of relationships and work will still sound thin, and equally abstract, unless contextualized by actual felt experiences of attachments and work enriched by the great metaphors of love and vocation that these traditions have delivered to us. It will be best if science aspires not to replace our spiritual traditions but to enrich and balance them.

The Double Entendre of Spiritual Language

There are dangers in giving too much play to the interaction among science, Protestantism, and modernization as functioning to push spirituality toward a more inner-worldly sensibility. The sense of transcendence could be lost and spirituality could gradually be seen only as a means to health, wealth, and general well-being. Science, especially, can have this impact. As Kenneth Pargament has astutely pointed out, most of the social sciences are undergirded by a form of philosophical pragmatism that measures human action, including religious action, in terms of its practical consequences for human health, wealth, education, and social productivity.[29] To help allay this possibility—this kind of narrowing of our spiritual sensibilities—I offer a recommendation. It has to do with the importance of maintaining the double entendre, the double meaning, of spiritual language.

To develop this point, I turn to some reflections by Philip Hefner, longtime editor of *Zygon*, the leading journal on science and religion. Hefner uncovers the double meaning of three New Testament terms central in Christian spirituality. In so doing, he may be giving us insights into how the inner-worldly and more transcendent aspects of spiritual language can be held together. The three Greek terms are *hiamonai*, which means to "heal or cure"; *therapeuo*, which means to "serve or care for"; and *sothesomai*, meaning to "make whole." Hefner points out: "These terms all share the character of the double entendre, that is, they refer to curing, caring, and wholeness as physical realities but also at the same time as spiritually transcendent meanings and realities."[30]

Here are some examples of what Hefner has in mind. In the Gospel of Matthew, we find the story of the centurion who asks Jesus to heal his servant who is "lying at home paralyzed, in terrible distress." Jesus immediately responds by saying, "I will come and cure him" (Matt. 8:7). This exchange seems to function at the level of physical cure. But then something happens to introduce a new level of meaning. The centurion confesses he is unworthy to have Jesus visit his house. Instead, he asks Jesus to use his powers to execute the cure from afar, as the centurion does when he gives orders to his troops. Jesus sees in the Roman centurion's response a great act of faith in who Jesus is—a faith that goes beyond anything he has otherwise found in all of Israel. This is an example of how an act of physical cure was also infused with the language of faith in a transcendent power.

For another example, take the word *sothesomai,* "to make whole." Hefner points out that "a cognate of this verb is the noun for 'savior.'" Hefner tells the story found in Matt. 9:18–26 about a woman suffering from a hemorrhage for twelve years who touched Jesus' cloak in hopes of being healed. Jesus immediately responded by saying, "Take heart, daughter; your faith has made you well" (v. 22). Even in this verse, the physical act of being made whole is mixed with a spiritual act of faith. But a few passages later, the double meaning of being physically whole and spiritually saved is emphasized even more when Jesus teaches, "For those who want to save their life will lose it, and those who lose their life for my sake will find it" (Matt. 16:25). Hefner points out that "the phrase 'save their life' contains the Greek word in question, and here it has a transcendent, spiritual meaning."[31]

My point here is that it is difficult to contain the language of healing, care, and wholeness within a strictly inner-worldly frame of reference. Most of us want bodily or psychological cure when we are ill, but it is difficult to conceive of our restoration in strictly physical or finite terms. What William James referred to as a sense of "more" and "overbelief" very easily slips into our consciousness and our language.[32] James located spiritual experience in our subconscious life; it was the source of our sense of "more"—our sense of powers beyond ourselves having effects on consciousness and actions. Freud would have called this more an unconscious identification with and projection of a parental imago.[33] Carl Jung would have explained it not as an identification with and project of the incest-prohibiting father but as a projection of various inherited archetypes, specifically the archetypal wish to be reborn.[34] Cognitive scientists of religion might call it a product of our folk psychological tendencies to assign agency to inanimate movements in the external world, which doubtless affect our inner life as well.[35]

Although James thought this sense of more was the source of spiritual life, he was even more interested in the over-beliefs attached to this sense of more. For him, these over-beliefs were our efforts to interpret and give meaning to this sense of more. James would agree with Ricoeur; our fascination with scientific explanation should not go so far as to trivialize the meanings and interpretations that communities and individuals have assigned to these over-beliefs. Toward the end of his *Varieties of Religious Experience* (1903), James writes:

> These ideas will thus be essential to that individual's religion—
> which is as much as to say that over-beliefs in various directions
> are absolutely indispensable, and that we should treat them
> with tenderness and tolerance so long as they are not intolerant
> themselves. . . . The most interesting and valuable things about
> a man are usually his over-beliefs.[36]

I must admit that I find both fascinating and disappointing much of what I read in the cognitive sciences about what some call HADD (Hyperactive Agency Detective Device)—the experimentally studied tendency of children and even older adults to attribute agency to movements by inanimate objects (such as clouds, falling rocks, lightning, and storms) and what this suggests about the possible origin of the idea of God or divine action. I feel as though I gain explanatory insight into the possible origins of our ideas about God or divine agency. But this research teaches me next to nothing about the various meanings or over-beliefs that people associate with their ideas about the divine. But, as we know, these ideas vary enormously in their respective meanings. And, as William James argued, they are not all equal in their *immediate luminosity, philosophical reasonableness,* and *moral fruitfulness*—his three great tests of the truth and value of religious experience and beliefs, tests that I will discuss more in the next chapter.[37]

So, to restate a central thesis of this book: it is important to keep the balance between our explanatory and interpretive interests so as not to lose the double entendres of spiritual life. We should pursue explanation but not so dogmatically as to lose interest in the various transcendent meanings of our religious and spiritual experience. This is especially true for those who have an interest in what I have argued is one of the most promising cultural contributions of the science-religion dialogue: the possible revival of religious humanism.

The Double Language of Psychology and Psychotherapy

Our science can attempt to suppress the "more" of our religious experience, but sometimes it creeps back and is evident in the very language of science. This is especially true in our psychological and psychotherapeutic disciplines. This is partially the case, I think, because in the end these disciplines contain practical, if not existential, interests that they do not always recognize. In my early work, I found a hint of a double language and some marks of spirituality in the way many secular psychotherapists spoke about the essential feature of the therapeutic relationship. At about the same time that I made these observations, theologian Thomas Oden saw much the same thing but accounted for what he observed in very different ways.

Carl Rogers's theory of therapeutic change gave me my initial insight, but I believe it can be seen in many forms of therapy. Rogers believed that all effective psychotherapeutic relationships need to communicate to the client both unconditional positive regard and empathy. A client is receiving unconditional positive regard if she perceives that of all her self-experiencing, none is judged by the therapist as "more or less worthy of positive regard."[38] Rogers defined empathy as a process of perceiving "the internal frame of reference of another with accuracy, and with the emotional components and meanings which pertain thereto, as if one were the other person, but without ever losing the 'as if' condition."[39] Together these two admittedly overly idealized formulations were thought to communicate a sense of acceptance to the client that was essential for relaxing his ego boundaries, experiencing himself more deeply, and sensing new possibilities for change as they emerged.

Expressed in very different words, we find much the same qualities of an effective relationship in Freud's concept of "evenly-hovering attention" designed to encourage and support the free association in the patient.[40] I believe it is evident in Alfred Adler's view that a good therapeutic relationship flows from the "social interest" of the therapist, which expresses itself in genuine interest "in the other" and the capacity to "see with his eyes and listen with his ears."[41] I could show a similar characterization of the therapeutic relationship in the writings of seemingly disparate therapists, such as Karl Menninger, Medard Boss, and the intriguing work of Carl Whitaker and Thomas Malone, as I showed in my early book *Atonement and Psychotherapy*.[42] Something quite close to Rogers's formulation can be found in the words of attachment therapist David Wallin when he writes that the therapists must have a "deliberate nonjudgmental attention to experience in the present moment—that is, a stance of mindfulness."[43] One cannot read the beautiful descriptions of the therapeutic empathy in the widely influential works of Heinz Kohut without believing that he, without ever saying it publicly, was on the same wavelength as his University of Chicago colleague Carl Rogers in believing that empathy communicated positive regard to the client as well.

But I am not here to endlessly elaborate these similarities between different schools of therapy. I am more interested in the deeper meaning surrounding this confluence of views. When it comes to Rogers's formulation, he explicitly believed that his two chief features of the good therapeutic relationship—unconditional positive regard and empathy—communicated to the client that he or she was a person of *worth* and *dignity*. Rogers acknowledged that this attitude was basically philosophical in nature. But he also thought it was the presupposition of a successful therapy.[44] It is my hunch that the analogues to Rogers's view of the essential elements in the therapeutic relationship found in other schools that we listed above also assume and communicate worth and dignity to the client.

But it was my view, and that of Oden, that Rogers and other therapists were saying more than they realized. We both believed that this affirmation of dignity and worth was an example of the double entendre of language that pervades much secular psychotherapy and personality theory and renders it more spiritual than is generally acknowledged. Furthermore, this double meaning may partially account for its effectiveness. Rogers is not just saying that this client is a person of worth and dignity to this particular therapist in this unique situation. He is also implying that the client is a person of worth and dignity more generally as a human being, not just to his or her individual therapist but in some deeper ontological sense. If this is true, then the therapist's individual unconditional positive regard and empathy does not itself grant this worth and dignity but recognizes and witnesses to a worth and dignity that are already there, possibly bestowed by some power or witness that transcends both therapist and client. If this is so, the finite acceptance of the therapist witnesses to a deeper level of acceptance that the client enjoys by the sheer fact of being human. To study the full fact of therapeutic change, the scientist might need to grasp both the small empirical structure of acceptance and the larger implied ontological structure and how they interact.

Thomas Oden invoked a specifically Christian, indeed christological, account of this deeper ontological affirmation of the client's worth and dignity. He grounded it in the nature of God revealed in Jesus Christ; in Christ, God is revealed as *"Deus pro nobis"*—God for us.[45] Oden gets this interpretation of Christ's revelation from the great mid-twentieth-century Swiss theologian Karl Barth. Barth's theology is itself a kind of evangelical Christian humanism that grounds the ontological dignity of persons in the Jewish and Christian God—the God who has, in fact, acted for all humankind. Oden boldly claimed that this act of God in Christ announced this message of all human ontological worth and is the unspoken presupposition of even the secular therapist's unconditional positive regard for the client. And this would be so for Oden even if the therapist never knew or acknowledged what God announced in Christ. This was the source of the larger implicit assumption about the ontological givenness of the client's dignity and worth. On a slightly different note,

Ricoeur, following Gadamer, might say that this revelation about the ultimate source of human worth revealed in Christ is simply a part of the effective history of the West and radiates out into the unconscious experience of limitless numbers of people, even the effective experience of both secular or religious psychotherapists.

On the other hand, back in the 1960s when this dialogue began, I drew from another source: the work of the great Whiteheadian philosopher of religion Charles Hartshorne. I followed Hartshorne in holding that this intuition about the client's fundamental dignity and worth was an intuition of general experience. And, yes, I too believed it implied a larger structure of power and meaning that was the origin of this worth. I held that the revelation of God in Christ itself witnesses to this more fundamental reality but is not the sole source of our insight.[46] Today, I would not so much reject my earlier Hartshornian account as supplement it with Ricoeur's hermeneutics and his use of Gadamer's understanding about how the classics of the past become part of our effective history, our actual experience, and our operative assumptions in ways we do not readily understand.

But my goal here is not to recapitulate the dialogue, and sometimes debate, that existed between Oden and me about how best to account for this larger source of affirmation of human worth. My goal is to point to at least one example in the therapeutic relationship itself of the interaction between explanation and understanding with regard to the grounds of the effective therapeutic change. This is the question as to whether the agent of change is the finite relationship or what it implies about some over-belief that testifies that neither a person's mother nor father, sister nor brother, shaman nor psychotherapist, is the exhaustive source of the client's worth but rather that some larger structure of meaning and being is this source. The dialogue between science and religion should both honor and study the interaction and importance of these two levels of significance. This will enhance the cooperation between science and religion and their possible contributions to a revived religious humanism.

Spirituality and Practical Reason

Early in this chapter, I argued that the scientific study of religion has influenced, along with other social factors, modern forms of spirituality toward more inner-worldly concerns with human connections, issues of work and vocation, and practical reason. So far, I have not talked about the new links between spirituality and practical reason. Much of the scientific work linking spirituality and practical reason has been suggestive but not definitive. Work on the benefits of mindfulness or even mystical experiences suggests that these states may contribute to loosening ego boundaries, disrupting rigid thought patterns, and thereby freeing practical reason to be more effective. But without more detailed work on the nature of practical reason, evidence that some spiritual experiences may make us freer and more flexible in our practical wisdom actually tells us little about their relationship.

It might help to examine some classical examples of the interaction of practical reason and spirituality. On this subject, I build once again on some insightful work by spirituality scholar Claire Wolfteich on the writings of Ignatius Loyola (1491–1556). Ignatius's life paralleled Luther's and Calvin's and was part of the Roman Catholic Counter Reformation.[47] He was born to a noble Spanish family with high aspirations for secular fame and honor. After being wounded in battle and following an intense period of reading and reflection, he wrote his famous *Spiritual Exercises* (1522) and used them to form the Society of Jesus, commonly referred to as the Jesuits.[48]

Ignatius's order was not modeled on the Benedictine emphasis on the cloister or the mendicant model of living off of alms. It emphasized more a life of service and the ordering of the priorities of life built on the goals of mission. Time and again, Ignatius recognized the inner-worldly goals of marriage and career—family and work—not unlike so many of the contemporary spiritualities. Ignatius seemed to understand that marriage and family as well as work and career would be natural pursuits for many people. He advised pursuing them, however, with an air of indifference so as not to become overly attached to these finite goods. Ignatius spoke of "disordered attachments," not unlike the attachment theorists of today. In order to keep our inner-worldly attachments from becoming disordered, Ignatius taught that there needed to be a proper order in our practical reason on the relation of means to ends.

Family and the benefits of work and career should be treated as finite and relative means that should be guided by a greater end. In one place, Ignatius writes:

> Hence, whatever I choose should help me to this end for which I am created, not ordering or drawing the end to the means, but the means to the end. Many persons first choose marriage, which is a means, and secondarily the service of God our Lord in marriage, though the service of God is the end. So also others first choose to earn an income, and afterwards to serve God through it. Such persons do not go directly to God, but want God to come to their disordered attachments. Consequently they make of the end a means, and of the means an end, so that what they ought to seek first, they seek last. Therefore my first aim should be to seek to serve God, which is the end, and only after that, if it is more profitable, to earn an income or to marry, for these are means to the end.[49]

This remarkable passage demonstrates a thick view of practical reason not far from the multidimensional view that I outlined in chapter 3 and associated with Ricoeur. Family and work become premoral goods that we are entitled to calculate about and pursue if we do so flexibly with a degree of detachment. At this level, Ignatius could have a conversation with Jonathan Haidt about the spirituality of human connections and work. But whereas Haidt pretty much makes human connections and work the ends of spirituality, Ignatius relativizes these goods to a higher principle: the service of God.

Ignatius would in fact be at odds with most of the modern scientific study of spirituality, which often measures it by the degree to which it serves what Ignatius would call the means of health, human connections, vocational success, and wealth rather than by some wider principle that would coordinate these relative goods in service of a higher and more general good.

But Ignatius's principle of service to God is actually thickened by the narrative that surrounds it. The exercises for weeks three and four of his program center around the narrative of the crucifixion and resurrection of Christ. Serving God—the principle that should guide our pursuit of the finite goods of family and work—meant for Ignatius recapitulating the story about the life, death, and resurrection of Jesus. But even then, Ignatius summarized the meaning of Jesus' life with a formulation of the meaning of Christian love—a formulation not unlike the principle of caritas that I wrote favorably about in chapter 2. The concrete meaning of glorifying God is a life lived according to mutual love. It is mutual love that should guide our pursuit of human connections and the rewards and meaning of our daily toil. And the rhythms of sacrifice and resurrection are implicit in the dynamics of mutual love. Ignatius wrote,

> Love consists in mutual sharing among persons, for example, as a lover gives and shares with the beloved what he or she possesses or has to give, and vice versa, the beloved shares with the lover. Thus if one has knowledge, it should be shared with one who does not, and so also with honors or riches, so that one is always sharing with others.[50]

I offer the example of spirituality from Ignatius as a case study in how spirituality and practical reason can work hand in hand. It is also a spirituality that affirms the finite goods of human connections and work. Ignatius orders these goods with a practical reason guided by the narrative of Jesus' life, death, and resurrection summarized by the principle of mutual love. It is this story, and the idea of mutual love, that transforms the quest for human connections into the mutual love of marriage, family life, and even a wider social philosophy. And it is mutual love that transforms our family and work life into a mission or vocation that also serves the greater good.

We must continue to read the classics of Western and world spirituality for what they contribute both to the realization of the finite goods of life and to their transformation into a wider and more general good for all. The tension between these two levels of meaning—this double entendre—is worthy of continued study and understanding by both the natural sciences and the normative disciplines of philosophy and theology.

5

Mental Health and Spirituality: Their Institutional Embodiment

Essential to the revival of a viable religious humanism is the institutional embodiment of religious experience and sensibility. It has been my thesis throughout this book that spirituality flourishes and endures best when it takes an institutional form with accompanying patterns of worship, ethics, corporate life, and service to the wider community. But the institutional embodiment of spirituality also must entail some degree of orchestration with the secular institutions of a society.

This is especially true and challenging for societies with advanced social systems that, as social theorists from Marx to Talcott Parsons have insisted, are chiefly characterized by the differentiation and relative independence of the various spheres of society.[1] So, when I use the word *orchestrate* to suggest what I have in mind, I mean that increasingly independent institutions of modern societies must work harder to position themselves conceptually in relation to other institutions that have different yet overlapping functions and goals. There always will be institutionally free-floating spiritualities in modern societies, and they will have their creative role to play. But the spirituality of modern societies must not be completely spontaneous, individual, and deinstitutionalized. Spirituality must have religious institutional embodiment to have a genuine and long-lasting impact on the lives of individuals and society.

The orchestration of the relation of institutions should also account for appropriate degrees of distance among them. Talcott Parsons understood this, even with regard to the role of the mental health disciplines. At the same time that he posited the need for a common value system at the highest symbolic level of a complex society that influenced the commitments of its more discrete sectors, he also saw the need for degrees of institutional independence.[2] This was especially true for psychotherapists, psychiatrists, and the mental health disciplines in general. When a client goes to a therapist, he does not expect the therapist to represent his father or mother. He wants a little distance from these family figures, not so much I would hope to become alienated from them as to gain the elbow room to sort out and improve his relationship to them. This is why Parsons believed in specialized pastoral counseling and pastoral psychotherapy. He believed that many troubled church people with psychological problems would do better with a counselor in a specialized setting who both had some degree of continuity with the beliefs, values, and symbols of the client's church and had some social distance from that confessing body as well. Parsons advanced a very convincing sociological justification for the rise of the modern-day pastoral counseling movement. Achieving this twofold position of continuity and differentiation by pastoral counselors with reference to church and family is an example of what I mean by institutional orchestration.

We do not currently talk much about the importance of institutions in either psychotherapy or spirituality. With the possible exception of family therapy, we do not develop theories of institutions in psychotherapy. Much of therapy is designed to help individuals rearrange their emotions in relation to various institutional attachments, especially family and job. Even in couple or family therapy, there is little work on the institution of marriage, the relation of marriage to the law, or even the legal and institutional aspects of family formation and dissolution. The same is true for our talk about spirituality. Although much spirituality is embodied in institutions—churches, temples, synagogues, denominations, and traditions with official leaders, doctrines, and systems of individual and social ethics—much of modern spirituality gets discussed and analyzed independently of institutional embodiments. So, without going so far as to say that either the mental health disciplines—psychology, social work, and psychiatry—or the new spiritualities are anti-institutional, it is safe to say that the theory and function of institutions are not central to their concerns.

But there are modern disciplines that are quite interested in the purpose and task of institutions. I am arguing that the mental health disciplines and the new interest in spirituality should be as well, as should the science-religion conversation that centers around these movements. Institutional theory should be a part of the science-religion discussion, especially if it is to contribute to a revived and socially effective religious humanism.

Because of my extensive work from the early 1990s to 2003 on the Religion, Culture, and Family Project at the University of Chicago, I increasingly became interested in the role of institutions—religious, legal, and economic—in shaping family formation and well-being. Although much of law itself—especially family law—is drifting into a kind of anti-institutionalism, several major theorists, including Milton Regan, Margaret Brinig, and Eric Posner, have developed elaborate theories about how institutions shape and stabilize individual, family, and group life—generally for the good.[3]

The University of Chicago is the home of individualistically oriented rational-choice economic theory associated with the name of Nobel Prize winner Milton Friedman. That theory was applied to the analysis of families by Gary Becker, another Nobel Prize winner, in his *Treatise on the Family* (1991).[4] The University of Chicago is also the home of what is called the new institutional economics, which celebrates the "signaling" and "channeling" and covenant-building functions of institutions—a school of economics associated with Nobel Prize winner Ronald Coase.[5] Coase's work is influencing family law, especially in the work of Margaret Brinig and her legal views of marriage, family formation, and what counts for child well-being.[6] Note that philosopher Kwame Appiah makes a very interesting observation in response to moral psychologists who claim that our moral decisions are primarily shaped by prereflective emotional intuitions with little influence from higher levels of deliberation. Even though Appiah is somewhat skeptical of such claims, he wisely points out that even if true, they might argue all the more for the importance of settled and tested institutions that would guide moral thinking on the basis of accumulated and examined experience.[7]

This chapter will argue for more reflection about the nature of institutions and their orchestration with regard to the mental health discipline of psychiatry and its relation to religion and culture. This issue too should be part of the conversation between religion and science. I will continue the institutional investigation in my concluding chapter on the relation of contemporary marriage and family therapy to present-day trends in family law.

The Crisis in Psychiatry

The struggle of psychiatry to define itself in relation to science, on the one hand, and culture, on the other hand, illustrates why institutional factors are so important in determining whether the science-religion dialogue will contribute to or detract from a revived religious humanism. Because psychiatry is a medical specialty practiced within the general field of medicine, it usually has assumed a vital tie between mental health and the body. But there are times when it has emphasized psyche more than body as the seat of mental health. Eric Kandel contends that prior to World War II, psychiatry in the United States was mainly rooted in biology. During and after World War II, it largely abandoned its biological roots, assimilated the insights of psychoanalysis, and adopted Freud's midcareer shift to interpretation and the efficacy of the talking therapies.[8]

Around the early 1980s, American psychiatry shifted once again from the psyche and moved toward the brain and body. Neuroscience is increasingly at the center of psychiatry. Jerrold Maxmen, in his *The New Psychiatry* (1985), announced that no longer were the psyche, problems of living, and the talking therapies at the core of psychiatry.[9] Psychiatry, he claimed, has lost interest in mental health. Rather, it is principally concerned with the treatment of mental disorders since, to be honest, nobody knows what mental health is.[10] He also claims that psychiatry is inept at addressing what is frequently referred to as "problems of living." Furthermore, as a professional specialty, he believes that psychiatry has no expert knowledge whatsoever about the purpose of life. Maxmen thought that psychopharmacology and the various versions of the DSM diagnostic codes have made psychiatry simultaneously more scientific and more humble. For psychiatrists, he claimed, the talking cures are only one among a battery of possible interventions. And Maxmen believed that psychiatrists were no better at addressing problems of living with psychotherapy than were psychologists, social workers, ministers, or maybe even bartenders.

In discussions with my psychiatric friends, I have come to believe that Maxmen is reasonably accurate in his description of the state of psychiatry today. It follows, then, that this medical specialty is left with two issues to face. First, if psychiatry is about mental disorders and not about mental health or happiness, how does it relate to these more positive goals for living? Second, how does psychiatry, with this more restricted self-understanding, relate to other institutions, such as religion, law, and moral systems, that have in the past addressed health, happiness and the purposes of life? I hold that it is not enough for psychiatry to follow Maxmen's renunciation of responsibility for these broader areas of life. The psychiatric profession has had enormous culture-making power. The frameworks that psychiatry uses to conceptualize their practices reflect back onto society, indirectly shaping understandings of life, its goals, and its purposes. It can renounce being the high priest of society defining health and happiness but nonetheless inadvertently still end by substituting new and untested views on these matters.

For instance, if the legal profession holds that law, like the marketplace, primarily should be ordered by rational-choice economic considerations, as held by the so-called law and economics school, then a calculative and material view of life may spread to those sectors of society touched by lawyers, courts, and legislatures, and from there to almost every nook and cranny of life. By analogy, if psychiatric practice reduces psyche to brain and biology, then this profession may unwittingly flatten life to these material forces, making both morality and religion difficult to conceptualize. This could happen even with Maxmen's generous gesture of referring most cases dealing with problems of living to nonmedical psychotherapists. Without developing understandings of health and the good life, how would psychiatry know whether to trust the contributions of other therapeutic resources?

In summary, Maxmen's solution leaves psychiatry without ways to position itself in relation to other institutions and traditions concerned with health and human purpose. In addition, since Maxmen wrote his book, psychiatry has spread its use of psychopharmacology beyond schizophrenia and clinical depression to additional forms of human stress by altering the functions of brains rather than by changing habits and attitudes toward life. The view of human nature assumed by this intervention may be spreading broadly throughout our society as well.

Difficulties with Humanistic Psychiatry

There are difficulties with a view of psychiatry—I suggest calling it humanistic psychiatry—that imagines it should directly address positive goals of life, such as health, happiness, and purpose. In various ways, this view made much of psychiatry into a positive culture with religious and ethical overtones, a role it was not philosophically prepared to assume.

I have argued elsewhere that Freud's near-cosmological theory of the life and death instincts bordered on a quasi-religious view of life; it contained images of the ultimate context of experience and implications for attitudes of skepticism and restraint that Philip Rieff summarized with the phrase "psychological man."[11] Erich Fromm had one of the most expansive views of psychiatry; his synthesis of psychoanalysis with the Frankfurt school's neo-Marxism would have made psychiatry into a social reform movement.[12] Erik Erikson's concept of mental health as "generativity" had strong resonances with positive models of moral selfhood found in the teleological tradition of philosophy associated with Aristotle and Thomas Aquinas.[13] Object relations theory in general, with the exception of Melanie Klein, seems riddled with deep metaphors suggesting that generosity and trust are at the core of human life. Heinz Kohut exhibited a similar ontology of trust in his later thinking. He believed that his self-psychology implied a view of life that he summarized with the concept of Tragic Man in contrast to Freud's Guilty Man.[14] Whereas Freud's Guilty Man implies a world of conflict and recrimination between the generations, Kohut's Tragic Man assumes a harmonious world of mutual self-actualization between the old and the young—a harmony similar to that found in most so-called humanistic psychologies.[15] I list these views not to attack them but to argue how easy it is for psychiatric concepts to slide over into ethics, ontology, quasi-religion, and positive philosophies for the guidance of society.

It is more difficult to avoid introducing into psychiatry implicit ontologies of life and views of human fulfillment than people like Maxmen tend to think. A psychiatry that claims to attend only to how the brain shapes moods and behaviors can easily end up suggesting that "nothing but" neurons influence feelings and actions. Furthermore, the belief that psychiatry is morally and metaphysically neutral can give rise to a kind of negative moral and religious nihilism that sets it at odds with Western cultural and religious resources. Unless psychiatry explicitly states that neuroscience cannot account for all of individual and social behavior, its silence on the additional factors that shape the psyche can imply that there is in fact nothing more. For psychiatry to remain silent on such matters is to contribute to reductionism by default.

Is Psychiatry Alienated
from American Religion?

Without addressing its relation—its orchestration—to American religious institutions, psychiatry risks alienating itself from American people and their religio-cultural traditions. Rather than encouraging the critical reappropriation of religious traditions in the form of a revived religious humanism, psychiatry in its new scientific narrowing may function to undermine religions and inadvertently contribute to hardening religious traditions into reactive and potentially destructive fundamentalisms. It can do this by simply allowing chemical and mechanical explanations of the mind to function as metaphors representing the final and determinative context of experience—allowing these concepts to symbolize all that there really is, all that really counts.

There is actual empirical evidence suggesting that American psychiatry's attitudes toward religion have contributed to alienating the profession from a significant portion of the American religious public. Research by psychiatrist David Larson and his associates shows that while as recently as the mid-1980s 90 percent of Americans believed in God, only 43 percent of American psychiatrists held those beliefs, even then a higher percentage than for psychologists and social workers.[16] Larson believed that such statistics suggest a significant cultural divide between psychiatry—and perhaps many U.S. mental health professions—and the general American population.

Furthermore, Larson's team found in a survey of over two thousand articles in four leading psychiatric journals between 1978 and 1982 that only fifty-nine papers contained a quantitative measure of religion and only three treated religion as a major emphasis. The small number of articles that did measure religions used "weak" or "static" measures, namely, the measure of denominational affiliation. These authors conclude that psychiatric theory during that period viewed religion "as a secondary derivative of structural psychic process."[17] In doing this, it tended to disregard more complicated models of religion found in the work of such scholars as Max Weber, William James, Clifford Geertz, Erik Erikson, Heinz Kohut, and Anthony Wallace.

Recent changes in the DSM-IV that take a more positive view of the possible adaptive potential of religious practices, as well as subsequent work by Larson and others on the contribution of spirituality to mental health, suggest that psychiatry may be changing its attitudes toward religion. I believe, however, that it still has a long way to go.[18] Hence, both at the level of practical attitude and at the level of scientific research, American psychiatry may be sowing unnecessary seeds of suspicion between itself and large sectors of the religious population that it hopes to serve. This may explain the rise of alternative religiously based systems of mental health delivery, such as Christian psychiatry, Christian psychotherapy, spiritually oriented psychological counseling, and specialized pastoral counselors. Such movements may be happening within the context of other religious traditions as well. People may be searching for mental health providers they can trust at the spiritual level.

Larson joined with such researchers as Harold Koenig and Michael McCullough to assess the health benefits of religion.[19] These investigations, still in their infancy but increasingly more sophisticated, should not be ignored by psychiatry in particular and by the public in general. If empirical research continues to show that people who understand themselves to be religious and who participate in religious institutions also have less depression, enjoy better life satisfaction in their work, have better interpersonal relations, are more generous with their philanthropy, volunteer their time more, live longer, and smoke and drink less or live longer even if they have these habits, then psychiatry in the name of promoting health would not want to do anything that would in principle alienate people from religion.[20] It might instead want to seek a variety of practical alliances with religion, especially in the mental health ministries of religious institutions.

Religious Humanism and a Public Philosophy for Psychiatry

If psychiatry needs to orchestrate its institutional life in relation to religion and its various institutional expressions, it should articulate a public philosophy. The purpose of this public philosophy would be to clarify psychiatry's self-definition and its relation to various aspects of society and culture, including their spiritual and religious dimensions. Whether psychiatry defines itself narrowly around mental disorder or broadly around health and fulfillment, it should locate its specialization in relation to other institutional spheres, such as law, ethics, and religion.

The idea of a public philosophy for psychiatry first emerged when I chaired a task force in the 1980s of psychiatrists, theologians, and historians on the topic of the relation of religion and psychiatry.[21] The vision of a public philosophy for psychiatry evolved from the deliberations, conferences, and books produced by this research group. The concept went beyond a code of professional ethics. Professional ethics governs the specific conduct of psychiatrists in relation to patients. But a public philosophy attempts to define the special focus and limits of psychiatry with reference to other spheres and activities of life. Of course, it was easier for the group to accept the need for such a philosophy than to articulate its actual substance. In some ways, at this early stage, the image of such a philosophy was more that of a public dialogue than any single unified stance. It was agreed, however, that progress was possible and that psychiatry's relation to religion should be one of its central interests because of their overlapping concerns with healing. Because of these shared commitments, the group believed that they would inevitably be seen as competitors, enemies, or friends. I further argued that such a philosophy should give reasons why psychiatry and religion should be collaborators in the revival of a contemporary religious humanism.

Can Hermeneutics and Pragmatism Be Sources?

What are some resources for a public philosophy for psychiatry? Here I return to my argument in chapter 1 that the dialogue between religion and psychology should proceed within the generous context of a critical hermeneutic philosophy that emphasizes the priority of understanding and the subordinate yet essential role for scientific distanciation and explanation. I relied most on Paul Ricoeur's enrichment of Gadamer's hermeneutic philosophy by building within it the necessity of natural-scientific distance and explanation. Starting with the priority of interpretation and understanding of the massive historical forces that have already formed us, I recommended resisting foundationalism as a philosophy to guide the science-religion conversation. I claimed that we can never reinvent the richness of our inherited cultural, ethical, and religious histories by forgetting this source and using science to create de novo our culture, morality, and worldview.

But in this chapter, I will supplement hermeneutic philosophy with American philosophical pragmatism. Pragmatism will help us mediate the explanatory findings of the natural and social sciences to the interpretive understanding of hermeneutics. How can this happen? How can pragmatism and hermeneutics live together to both inform the religion-science conversation and help develop a public philosophy for psychiatry? Answering this question is the purpose of the remaining paragraphs of this chapter.

It can be argued that all American psychiatrists are philosophical pragmatists in their hearts. Pragmatism better than other philosophies probably best accounts for the judgments made in the clinical psychological disciplines. As was the case with Charles Pierce, William James, and John Dewey, American psychiatrists are interested in how theory affects experience, especially the experience of patients. Pragmatists believe cognitive knowledge and moral knowledge emerge out of practice and return to and are tested by the realities of practice.

For the purposes of my argument about how pragmatism and hermeneutics can inform a public philosophy for psychiatry, I am mainly interested in pragmatism's views of religion, especially those developed by William James. James's philosophical approach to religion offers much to psychiatry and can also help bridge the space between hermeneutics and pragmatism, between explanation and interpretation, between functionalism and understanding. James teaches that it is philosophically more sound to be interested in the consequences of religion than in its origins. In the first chapter of *The Varieties of Religious Experience* (1903), James admits that many forms of religious experience seem to be associated with pathological psychological states, developmental disorders, and sexual conflicts.[22] Had he been alive today, he probably would have included Freud's wish fulfillment, cognitive science's interest in our so-called Hyperactive Agency Detection Device (HADD), or the neural changes associated with mystical or transcendent experiences of the kind investigated by Andrew Newberg. But James claimed that the causal factors, which may in part shape the origins of any human experience (including religious experience), do not constitute the philosophical grounds upon which the value and truth of that experience can be judged.[23] James used the term *medical materialism* for the view that a religious experience is "nothing but" its prima facie causal conditions, which may appear to scientists as originating in developmental conflicts, neurological errors, or observable changes in the brain. He found this kind of reductionism quite prevalent in the psychiatric practice of his day; we see both hard and soft forms of it even in our own time, especially in those scientific endeavors most influenced by psychopharmacology and in some, though certainly not all, forms of cognitive neuroscience.

James first of all approached religion with his own brand of phenomenology. As I pointed out in chapter 1, it was not Gadamer's or Ricoeur's brand of phenomenology. From their perspectives, James would be viewed as neglecting a description of the role of myth, metaphor, symbol, narrative, and history in mediating religious experience. However, historical research has now demonstrated that James was a major source for the phenomenological philosophy of Edmund Husserl and thereby the entire European existential-phenomenological movement that Husserl indirectly inspired.[24] In this way, James is in the dim background of Gadamer and Ricoeur as well.

It has frequently been overlooked that James's pragmatic approach to religion was built on a nonreductive phenomenological beginning point; psychiatry should notice that he began his analysis of religion simply by describing as thoroughly as possible the thick sense of "objective presence" and meaning that accompanies most religious experience.[25] James did not overlook the psychologically and even neurologically conditioned states of religious experience, but he never treated them as exhaustive causal accounts of religious phenomena. Although the full scope of psychodynamic interpretations of religion was not available to James, we can be certain he would have used them, but never in ways that unseated his first concern to describe religion phenomenologically.

But James was just as interested in assessing the consequences of religious experience as he was in describing the experience itself. This is where we see his pragmatism in full force. But before examining the consequences of religious or spiritual experience, he treated the experience phenomenologically. Bear this point in mind. This is the difference between James's functionalism and so many other functionalist options in the social sciences. Furthermore, he developed powerful philosophical reinforcements to support his phenomenology. James located the descriptive or phenomenological moment of handling religion under the rubric of what he came to call "radical empiricism."[26] He took experience seriously. Experience in the radical sense was for him first of all a complex web of felt meanings rather than sense impressions, as it was for Locke; external reinforcements, as it later was for B. F. Skinner; or neural firings, as it is for some neuroscientists.

James's philosophical pragmatism, however, is distinguishable from his radical empiricism. His pragmatism assumed his radical empiricism and its respect for the phenomenological beginning point. But his pragmatism as such was actually more concerned with the consequences of our propositions about and interpretations of these experiences. James was particularly interested in the consequences of claims, propositions, and interpretations of religious experiences. His radical empiricism allowed him to describe religion nonreductively; his pragmatism made him interested in the practical truth of religion (that is, its web of consequences in enhancing a range of other goods, such as health, a sense of security, wealth, and general well-being). His pragmatism influences the philosophical background of much of our social-science study of religion today.

James had a threefold test for the value and truth of religious experience that a public philosophy for psychiatry should keep in mind. The three criteria or tests for the truth and value of religious experience were "immediate luminousness," "philosophical reasonableness," and "moral fruitfulness."[27] James actually held that these three criteria make up what he called our "spiritual judgments." The immediate luminousness of the experience counts for something in the evaluation of religion; if people claim their religion enlightens them, this testimony should be taken seriously as one important aspect of the assessment. In addition, the immediacy of the experience is where James's brand of phenomenological psychology comes to bear. The immediate testimony of these experiences— their meaning and illumination—should be for both social scientists and psychiatry descriptive beginning points in their study as well as a criterion for evaluating their possible truth and value.

But the criterion of immediate luminosity is not sufficient. A public philosophy struggling to relate itself to religious claims and institutions would not find that sufficient in and of itself. It must be supplemented by a second test—the general philosophical reasonableness of the religious claim, that is, its consistency with other commonly accepted states of knowledge, which James at one place calls "the rest of what we hold as true."[28] This principle should not be read in a foundationalist manner. The rest of what we hold as true is not to be viewed as immutable a priori truths or the irrefutable findings of experimental science. In James's view, this has more to do with our fund of more or less experientially tested and assumed hypotheses about how the world and society work. When claims based on spiritual experience go too far beyond this commonly accepted fund of hypotheses, James would say that there are grounds to be skeptical.

Moral fruitfulness—James's third criterion—is the most important for a public philosophy for psychiatry. With regard to a religious experience or claim, here we are asked to weigh "not its origin, but the way in which it works on the whole."[29] In James, phenomenology and functionalism are joined. He holds together the concern to describe experience nonreductively (the phenomenological move) and the concern to assess how the experience functions in individual and communal life (the functional move). This happens because of his insistence that a religious experience should not too rapidly be reduced to its associated conflicts, pathologies, human needs, human wants, or correlated brain states.

What, however, does moral fruitfulness mean more specifically? In making the moral a partial judge of the religious, James took a step in the direction of Kant and most of modern liberal thought about religion. But because he held moral fruitfulness in tension with immediate luminousness and philosophical reasonableness, he did not reduce all evaluation of religion to the moral point of view. In addition, James had a much richer concept of the moral than did Kant, one much closer to Ricoeur's emphasis on the priority of the good over the right, of ethics over morality, or, as Louis Janssens would say, the priority of the premoral in relation to the more fully moral. James saw ethics as guiding the actualization of fundamental psychobiological needs. But humans have more needs, both high and low needs, than can be easily organized with one another.

On this point, I think James would agree with moral intuitionists such as Jonathan Haidt and Joshua Greene; being the evolutionary thinker that he was, he would have little trouble with the idea that humans have very primitive intuitions about such things as good, bad, danger, purity, and disgust. But he also would reassert his main point: our needs and various primitive evaluations can and do conflict. Therefore deliberation as well as society's inherited ethical systems are needed to hierarchicalize these moral intuitions so that the more efficacious ones are held supreme and expressed in ways that are compatible with the needs of other people and society as a whole.

This last concern made justice central to morality for James, just as it was for Kant. But James advocated a justice that guided the satisfaction of human needs and desires and the realization of human flourishing. It was, indeed, a kind of religious humanism. Or, to use Ricoeur's concept, justice guides and critiques our teleological search for the goods of life. From the perspective of the interests of psychiatry as profession and institution, justice as James saw it helps actualize mental and physical health. But, by the same token, health for James is never completely disconnected from justice nor allowed to trump it. The religious experience of individuals should be evaluated not by its origins but by its consequences, and these consequences should be judged in part by the degree to which they shape the whole moral pattern of a person's life as he lives with others so that all people can justly fulfill their respective needs as well.

James's perspective on religion, especially when supplemented with Ricoeur's more mature hermeneutic phenomenology, can contribute to a public philosophy for psychiatry in its need to articulate its attitude toward religion. It helps answer the charge that one psychiatrist recently made to the senior psychoanalyst in his community: "You know, of course, that this religion stuff is all garbage." The senior analyst did not agree, although he was fully aware that sometimes religion can become distorted. He confided to me that, in his judgment, it goes far beyond the epistemological competence of psychiatry as a profession to make the metaphysical judgment that it is all useless fantasy or to make the moral judgment that all religion is pernicious. James can help psychiatry resist these intellectual traps, which could easily spread from the books of the so-called new atheists to the helping disciplines, including psychiatry.

James's respectful attitude toward religion also makes sense clinically. How is this so? Both James and Kant could agree that respecting persons gets to the core of moral behavior. Without invoking Kant or James, many modern psychotherapists also are aware that respect for persons when dynamically mediated gets to the heart of psychological cure—a point I made in my discussion of Rogers, Freud, Kohut, and others in chapter 4. Many modern therapists have unknowingly turned Kant's imperative to treat persons as ends and never only as means into a strategy of cure. But if respect is to be administered psychodynamically and to be more than a vague attitude, it must be shown, as Paul Ricoeur has argued, concretely with reference to the person's narrative self—a person's identity or story that she tells about herself, with all of its introjects, attachments, and conflicting needs and selves. And frequently, a crucial aspect of a person's narrative identity is her religious experience. Hence, respecting the self of a patient should also entail respecting her conscious or unconscious religious identity, even if one later also helps assess its consequences in her life.

Narrative Identity and the Religious

The idea of narrative identity is a relatively new concept in philosophy. It also can be found in psychoanalysis, moral psychology, and the personality theories of Dan McAdams and John Kotre.[30] It suggests that a person is defined not only by the abstract qualities of freedom and self-transcendence, as Kant contended, but also by the stories or narratives that he tells about himself and the way they consciously and unconsciously organize needs, attachments, and a person's various social selves.

This is why one of the most effective ways to show respect for another person is to allow him to talk about himself (that is, to tell his story). For vast numbers of Americans, as well as people throughout the world, religion is a conscious part of that story, even if they are not participants in religious institutions. Whether a patient or client is more spiritual than religious or locates her spirituality within an institutional context, psychiatry must know when it should listen to that spiritual or religious story, describe it phenomenologically as James suggested, but also trace its consequences, which sometimes are productive but sometimes not.

Ann Marie Rizzuto, in her important book *Birth of the Living God* (1979), argues that all people construct images of the divine during childhood that are complex syntheses of parental and sibling internalized images.[31] Some people repress these images and disconnect them from culturally mediated images of the divine. This may be especially prevalent in more secular societies. These people think that they are atheists or agnostics when at the unconscious level they still carry images of their childhood God. Others later in their lives bring these primitive images into interaction with the classic images of the divine mediated by a society's enduring religious institutions.[32] In many instances, these are the persons whose religious identities mature and function to guide them to both healthy and morally responsible living.

A psychiatrist once confessed to me that he had an absolutely wretched childhood with highly ambivalent, rejecting, and neglectful parents. By accident, he began reading the Bible. The image of God the father and parent he found in the New Testament was in stark contrast to the qualities he found in his parents. At one point he said to me, "God became my parent." To use Ricoeur's formulation, which he worked out so well in *Freud and Philosophy* (1970), this psychiatrist brought the "archeology" of his own inadequate parental imagos to the "teleology" of the New Testament picture of parenthood that gradually over time restructured his own primitive introjections.[33]

Rizzuto's insights into how our unconscious images of the divine can interact with culturally mediated images are consistent with the views of James. Both treat these cultural images phenomenologically, just as Ricoeur treats phenomenologically what he calls cultural "figures of the spirit," which most of us carry in our psyches and that are deposited there by our effective histories—cultural stories and images that we hardly know we have internalized in addition to our images of our parents.[34]

In fact, both Rizzuto and Ricoeur surpass James in their capacity to hold in dialectical tension phenomenological descriptions of religious experience with psychodynamic explanations of our archaeologies—our affectively cathected parental and familial introjects. In doing this, these two philosophers contribute to a public philosophy for psychiatry in its relation to religion. Rizzuto and Ricoeur do not reduce all religion to our unconscious projections, but they help us see how our culturally mediated religious ideas and practices often interact with, embellish, and redirect childhood religious ideation. A similar view, relying more on the work of Heinz Kohut and Donald Winnicott than Ricoeur or Rizutto, can be found in James Jones's *Contemporary Psychoanalysis and Religion* (1991).[35] Jones argues for a relational view of religious experience in which the projected needs of the individual and culturally mediated images of the divine are both allowed to have a voice in the psychiatrist's interpretations.

Psychiatry needs a public philosophy, or at least an ongoing conversation about such a philosophy. This public philosophy, among other tasks, should provide frameworks for psychiatry as an institution in relation to other institutions of society, including religion in both its institutional and less structured forms. Achieving this will contribute much to a mutually reinforcing relation between psychiatric and religious institutions that will constitute one part of the emergence of a revived religious humanism. Of course, religious institutions should develop their own public philosophy of institutional relations. Much of what I have argued in this book should help with this. In the next chapter, I will discuss more about why the science-religion conversation needs to attend to institutional theory.

Institutional Ethics and Families: Therapy, Law, and Religion

In the course of this book, institutional aspects of the science-religion dialogue have become increasingly salient. This is especially true for the dialogue among psychology, psychotherapy, and religion because of the direct cultural and social impact of each of these practices and disciplines.

We first touched on the importance of institutions in Kwame Appiah's response to the emphasis by leading moral psychologists Joshua Greene and Jonathan Haidt on the priority of moral intuitions in contrast to moral deliberation as emphasized by Kant or the utilitarian John Stuart Mill. Appiah acknowledged that spontaneous moral intuitions about pleasure and pain, danger and safety, purity and disgust, and in-group versus out-group may be basic to our moral responses. But he does not rule out a role for moral deliberations. To be honest, neither do moral psychologists Greene and Haidt. Rather, they tend to relegate deliberation to impersonal moral decisions pertaining to public policy or larger groups rather than personal moral decisions where we live most of our moral lives.[1] These moral psychologists also claim that these different moral responses are located and controlled by different parts of the brain.

In acknowledging the possible truth of these observations, Appiah, as we have seen, goes one step further and suggests that such insights really argue for the importance of institutions—institutions, I take it, established by long-term deliberative processes by groups that have been tested, often revised over time, and that also help guide both personal and public decisions. This is close, as I have observed, to Ricoeur's understanding of the important role of inherited classic practices, which should be understood as institutional practices as well.

Appiah's astute observation suggests that there may be more room for models of moral reflection associated with the cognitive theories of Lawrence Kohlberg and the closely associated discourse ethics of Jürgen Habermas than the work of Greene and Haidt seem to imply.[2] Of course, in view of recent advances in understanding the role of emotions in ethics and morality, the reigning models of moral thinking for the future will be what is often called "mixed deontological" models of the kind *not* fully found in Kohlberg or Habermas.[3] These are models of moral thinking that emphasize the priority of emotional intuitions toward the premoral goods of life—as we saw in Frankena, Janssens, and Ricoeur—but are finally organized both by our higher deliberative capacities and by more tested traditions of moral deliberation generally taking the form of inherited but evolving institutional patterns.

The second place the institutional question emerged was in our discussion of psychiatry and its relation to other institutions, especially religious institutions. I argued that there is a need for a public philosophy for psychiatry that would help orchestrate its relation to other institutions, including law, the nonmedical mental health professions, and spirituality in both its more free-floating and institutional forms. A public philosophy for psychiatry would have both clinical implications for how religion is treated and cultural implications for how psychiatry is perceived by the larger society and its capacity to cooperate with other institutions.

I will now apply that discussion to a specialty in both psychiatry and the other mental health disciplines: the practice of family and marriage psychotherapy and counseling.

The Ethics of Family
and Marriage Counselors

American psychotherapy and counseling has been criticized for promoting an individualistic ethic of personal satisfaction and variously defined understandings of individual self-fulfillment. As I have pointed out in earlier chapters, Robert Bellah, Christopher Lasch, and more recently the team of Frank Richardson, Blaine Fowers, and Charles Guignon have all advanced this criticism. I have been a part of this critique as well, as I confessed in chapter 3. All of these analyses, including my own, have been cultural reviews of the therapies based primarily on the written texts of their principal leaders. It should be acknowledged that even though this is one way to grasp the cultural implications of these movements, this does not get to the self-image of individual therapists about the moral meaning of their work. Nor does it capture what is actually done in the counseling process, which may not be nearly as individualistic as these critics have said. Finally, the cultural critiques for the most part lumped all the psychotherapies together, failing to make simple distinctions between individual therapy and marriage and family counseling and therapy.

From 1991 to 2003, I directed at the Divinity School of the University of Chicago the Religion, Culture, and Family Project, which was generously funded by a series of grants from the Division of Religion of the Lilly Endowment. We produced two series of books[4] as well as a PBS documentary and accompanying book called *Marriage: Just a Piece of Paper?* The documentary showed on stations throughout the country during the spring of 2002.[5] We also conducted two empirical studies pertaining to the family field, one involving a national survey of models of love that people believe correlate with a good marriage[6] and one on the ethical convictions of marriage and family therapists. I want to tell you about the latter study.

During the mid-1990s, I joined with colleagues in family therapy and a statistician to execute a major national survey of the ethical commitments of marriage and family counselors and therapists. It reached publication in the professional journal *Family Relations.*[7] We sent the survey to 2,500 marriage and family therapists who identified themselves as members of one or more of five professional organizations: American Association of Marriage and Family Therapy (AAMFT), American Psychological Association (APA), American Psychiatric Association (APA, MD), National Association of Social Workers (NASW), and American Association of Pastoral Counselors (AAPC). We received 1,035 completed surveys—a robust 41 percent of the original mailing—with responses fairly evenly divided among the five professions.

The punch line of the results of this survey should not be too surprising, but it does correct the prevailing image held in many circles about the individualistic—maybe even ethical egoist—goals of the modern psychotherapies. Marriage and family therapists and counselors hold more communal, relational, and traditional values of the purposes of their work than is implied in the critiques of Bellah, Lasch, Richardson, and my own early work. They hold less individualistic views than the official professional code of ethics of all these organizations, codes that tend to emphasize Kantian-like respect for the dignity and autonomy of the individual counselee over all other values.[8]

Although no universally shared ethic exists among these therapists, a significant portion of counselors and psychotherapists do hold a dominant ethic, an ethic that if brought forth and systematized could form the outlines of a public philosophy for this specialty of therapy and counseling. It could help dispel misperceptions of the mental health disciplines, at least in this area of family and couples work. It could orchestrate their work with other institutional sectors of society, especially the religious sphere but, as we soon will see, with contemporary family law as well.

According to the small number of professional articles that exist on the ethical sensibilities of marriage and family therapists, proposals about an adequate ethic have oscillated between individualistic or autonomy-oriented ethics and a systems view that emphasizes the good of the family group as a whole over the good of the individual.[9] Neither of these views seems quite accurate when compared to the self-understanding of the thousand-plus respondents to our survey.

A significant portion seemed to hold an ethic of what we called "relationality"—an ethic that emphasizes affection and empathy among family members and that both respects individuals and meets their needs as well as fostering mutuality and justice among all family members.[10] We saw this ethic at several points in the responses we received to our survey. When we asked the therapists about what they held to be the "good moral life," 40.2 percent answered "creating and fostering loving and caring relations" followed by a 23.85 percent rate for another highly relational and, I might add, somewhat deontological principle of the Golden Rule—"acting toward others as you would ideally wish them to act toward you."[11] These answers trumped far more individualistic formulations of the good moral life, such as "being true to the unfolding potential of one's inner self" and increasing the good of the individual self without directly harming another—which yielded 14.7 percent and 5.8 percent of the responses, respectively. Low on the totem pole was the divine command formulation that the good moral life was a matter of "following the will of a higher power" (13.2 percent) and the thought-to-be popular utilitarian "doing the most for the largest number of people" (2.1 percent). It is interesting to notice that, at this more abstract level of a general ethic toward life, there was little difference in the responses of male and female therapists.[12]

When we asked more concretely what was the "purpose of families," the two relational choices of "families are for mutual support and practical helpfulness" (54.2 percent) and "families are for friendship and sharing" (17.3 percent) constituted a whopping 71.5 percent. The choice "families are for having and socializing children" was third, at an overall 19.3 percent, with more men therapists (22.6 percent) than women therapists (14.6 percent) affirming that purpose as central to what families are about. Once again, the idea that "families are for individual members" came in last, at 6 percent of the respondents.[13]

The more concrete the questions got, the more surprising the answers. When we asked, "Are some family forms more health promoting for children?" 58.9 percent said yes and 41.1 percent said no. But this somewhat conservative-sounding response got larger when we asked some additional questions. Of those therapists who thought family form made a difference for children, 70.4 percent thought that the "traditional working father and mother at home with children" was superior. This was followed by "two-income husband-wife nuclear family" at 25 percent and blended families, single parents, and gay and lesbian couples at 2 percent, 1.4 percent, and 1.1 percent, respectively.[14] On divorce, 61.1 percent said that they were in their therapeutic practice "neutral on divorce and do what is best from a therapeutic point of view." But this was quickly followed by a significant 33.3 percent who said they were "committed to preserving marriage and avoiding divorce whenever possible." Only 2.4 percent would admit that they "often recommend divorce when it is psychologically best for the individuals."[15]

There is much more in the report, but you have doubtless had enough statistics for right now and probably have a taste for why it contrasts with some of the overly broad cultural analyses of the individualistic ethical implications of the psychotherapies. In fact, some of the commonalities in ethics among these diverse groups of family therapists may contain the nuggets of a public philosophy for this loose consortium of mental health specialists. In addition, this report contains implications for the larger normative themes running through this book. Remember, I have said that the science-religion dialogue may have the function of reviving a religious humanism. I have tried to illustrate this with comments about Christian humanism. This empirical study may also have implications for the humanistic dimension of religion as well.

One issue that I discussed in chapter 2 was the definition of Christian love and the relative validity of the competing agape, caritas, and eros views. Influenced in part by currents in contemporary social neuroscience and moral psychology, I built the case for a strong role for the affections in ethics and morality guided by an ethic of equal regard and ended by arguing for the superiority of the caritas model. The emphasis on affection, empathy, and mutuality in the marriage and family therapists' ethic of relationality is one more example of how the science-religion conversation can help revive a Christian humanism as well as give more prominence to the caritas view of Christian love. In light of the ethical options competing in family therapy, the relational view is closer to caritas than are either the ethic of individualism or the strong system ethic that subordinates individual need to the health of the family as a whole. Caritas, as you recall, builds on our natural affections—especially for our offspring—even as it gradually extends these affections to others.

The Case of Psychology, Biology, and Evolutionary Theory

This survey helps soften charges against the modern therapies that they err in the direction of an ethic of individualism. But an ethic of relationality can give rise to its own misunderstandings. It may be seen to overemphasize process, affection, and communication in contrast to deeper bio-economic functions of families as well as religious elements of blessing and covenant. Remember that having and socializing children was relatively low in these therapists' list of the purpose of families. This may possibly contradict their rather strong views that not all family forms are equal for the good of children and that families with traditional bread-earner fathers and stay-at-home mothers are better for child rearing than the dual-income nuclear mother-father arrangement, which was ranked a distant second. This lack of attention by family therapists to bio-economic factors—what I call, following Ricoeur's theory of symbolism, an "archeology" of human motivation[16]—does not correspond to the preoccupations of the rest of the social sciences, let alone the history of marriage and family in the great religions, including Christianity. The relation of families and marriage to child well-being, poverty, health, and general human health are dominant concerns of both of these traditions of inquiry, that is, the social-science disciplines of economics, sociology, and biology and, on the other hand, the great religious traditions.

We first ran into the more bio-economic view in reference to social neuroscientist John Cacioppo in chapter 2. Building on the work of William Hamilton's theory of inclusive fitness and Robert Trivers's views on the biology of parental investment, Cacioppo has advanced the hypothesis well-grounded in evolutionary theory that "motives toward inclusive fitness and kin altruism are the core of human intergenerational care and the vital link between sociality and spirituality."[17] According to Cacioppo, this is because to live on in our offspring requires not only that we have children but that our children have children. For this to happen, there must be a great deal of long-term investment by parents and even extended family and the wider community, thereby building a web of sociality that binds intergenerational community together. The long period of human infant dependence, in contrast to other species, is the key that pressures humans to form both long-lasting marital unions and supportive communities to ensure that offspring endure.

The second time we ran across this pattern of thinking was in the positive psychology of Jonathan Haidt, who repeated Cacioppo's line of argument almost exactly but with no reference to him. This only shows how widespread this form of thinking is for those disciplines that draw on evolutionary theory. Recall that Haidt's thoughts on these matters emerged in his discussion of happiness and how important—as social neuroscientist Cacioppo also believed—attachments are to happiness. As you would expect, the work of John Bowlby and Mary Ainsworth have been important resources for Haidt's thinking. But then he went a step further. He agrees with Cacioppo and many other evolutionary thinkers that it is the large brains and heads of human infants leading to their early birth and long period of helplessness that binds human fathers and mothers together in ways not found in other species. As Haidt says, this accounts for why "a universal feature of human cultures is that men and women form relationships intended to last for years (marriage) that constrain their sexual behavior and institutionalize their ties to children and to each other."[18]

The third time in this book that we encountered this bio-economic archeology of the institution of marriage came from the thirteenth-century Roman Catholic Thomas Aquinas when he wrote:

> There are animals whose offspring are able to seek food immediately after birth, or are sufficiently fed by their mother; and in these there is no tie between male and female; whereas in those whose offspring needing the support of both parents, although for a short time, there is a certain tie, as may be seen in certain birds. In man, however, since the child needs the parents' care for a long time, there is a very great tie between male and female, to which tie even the generic nature inclines.[19]

So, to work out their mutual and long-term inclusive fitness, the attachment of human parents to their highly dependent human infants and children becomes central, so important that family formation has included the male at the human level. Haidt then adds another wrinkle, one quite familiar to both individual and family therapists and one turned into a therapeutic empire in the school of imago therapy founded by Harville Hendrix.[20] This is the insight that humans, in contrast to other species, recapitulate their parent-child attachments—avoidant, secure, or ambivalent, to use the refinements of Ainsworth[21]—into their relationships with their mates. Patterns of childhood attachments become part of an intergenerational web of sociality that stretches throughout, and perhaps beyond, a single individual's human life cycle.

But, as we will soon see, the institutionalization of this web of attachments in family formation and marriage is very much at risk in modern societies. This is not due just to the dynamics of modernization, although these are certainly significant contributors. It is partially the consequence of a move in family law itself to deinstitutionalize marriage, a move that can be discussed without any reference to the controversial debates storming around the question of same-sex marriage. And the modern psychologies inform these movements depending on which of the various schools of thought and research are taken seriously by contemporary legal theorists. So the question of the institutional orchestration of law and family psychotherapy is the matter at stake in the discussion that follows.

The Case of Law: Close Relationships, Channeling, and Bio-Economics

The dominant trend in family law theory today is toward what is commonly called the principle of "private ordering." One can find this principle developed in a variety of prominent sources in family legal theory, including the writings of Martha Ertman,[22] Daniel Friedman,[23] the prestigious American Law Institute's (ALI) proposed reformation of U.S. family law in its voluminous *Principles of the Law of Family Dissolution* (2002),[24] and the Canadian Law Commission's *Beyond Conjugality* (2001).[25] Private ordering means that law and society should support the individual decisions of citizens in the area of sexuality, family formation, and procreation without the guidance and constraints of settled law.[26] The assumption behind this idea is that individuals have the moral capacity and understanding to make good judgments about their needs and situations in the area of intimacy and procreation better than do government, legislators, and the law. The principle also implies that, although law should do little to constrain private ordering, law and government should be willing to support its consequences with welfare grants and flexible legal provisions handling the new challenges of child custody, definitions of legal parenthood, and visitation rights emerging from the increase of divorce, out-of-wedlock births, cohabitation, and the wider use by unmarried couples and singles of the advances in assisted reproductive technology (ART).

The new respect in legal theory for the principle of private ordering expresses itself in a variety of proposals. In the American Law Institute's recommendations, it takes the form of total neglect of the law of family formation while concentrating the resources of the law and its courts primarily on the law of the dissolution of families. At the same time, the report—revealingly titled *Principles of the Law of Family Dissolution*—renders cohabitation and marriage virtually equivalent before the law by applying marriage law to cohabitors when these couples break up.[27] Accommodation to private ordering also shows up in its interpretations of the best interests of the child in situations of family dissolution. In an effort to provide continuity for the child in complex situations where the child may have had a variety of caretakers in fluid and informal family constellations, the *Principles* would extend visitation rights and even legal parenthood to three, four, or potentially more adults in the child's life.[28]

Other interesting proposals are being advanced. Emory University's legal scholar Martha Fineman recommends going further and delegalizing marriage completely. Marriage as such—or what she calls the "sexual family"—should be of no interest to the law.[29] What requires legal involvement, support, and coercion are actual dependency cases—a single mother caring for her children, a middle-aged son or daughter caring for an elderly parent, two elderly sisters or perhaps just friends who depend on each other during moments of infirmity.[30] Fineman contends that these are the kinds of dependency arrangements that today require the supports and benefits we once gave to marriage. She holds that if married couples want the protections of law, they can develop private contracts that courts could respect in times of conflict.[31] If couples want the comforts of religious marriage, they can turn to the customary rituals of their respective religious traditions. But these ceremonies would have no status as such before the law.

It is important for us not to lose track of the main point of this discussion. This is the point of institutional orchestration between marriage and family therapists and other institutions—in this case, the law. Would marriage and family therapists have, individually or as professional groups, thoughts about these proposed reforms? What would they think about other prominent recommendations? Take the interesting reforms advocated by June Carbone, a legal scholar at the University of Missouri. In her book *From Partners to Parents* (2000), Carbone does not go as far as Fineman toward delegalizing marriage.[32] But she does believe that because of the extensive changes in sexual patterns in modern societies, marriage as an institution can no longer be relied upon to define and order the responsibilities of parenthood. [33] According to her, defining and reinforcing parenthood should now become the main preoccupation of family law. Carbone's proposals to legally disconnect marriage and parenthood are summarized forcefully in the following quote.

> Early modern and Victorian societies provided for children through marriage. The marital link, which defined "legitimacy," provided clear lines of connection and responsibility. And when marriage itself changed from an arranged affair to one based on choice, internalized gender roles served to link the voluntary institution to social obligations—chief among which were obligations to children. Lawrence Friedman's "republic of choice" provides no such automatic connections. Sex need not indicate openness toward parenthood; parenthood creates no obligation to marry; marriage implies no particular organization for meeting the needs of children.[34]

Carbone proposes making parenthood, in contrast to marriage, the new status before the law, a status that would replace the privileges and responsibilities customarily enjoyed by giving marriage a special legal status. By the idea of status, the law means a predefined legal category that is not amenable to individual contractual negotiations. Marriage historically has had many of these predefined characteristics. Parenthood did too when it was tied to marriage. Now, Carbone wants parenthood to have this legal status independently of marriage. She writes:

If family obligation is to be rebuilt on lines of status—indeed, if it is to be rebuilt at all in a way that links individual obligation to societal needs—then parenthood may be the only remaining candidate. Parenthood may play the part marriage once did of initiating young men and women into a socially sanctioned role whether or not they would voluntarily embrace all of the role requirements.[35]

The doctrine of private ordering would be a bit more constrained in Carbone than it would be in Fineman. It would not so easily be applied to parenthood, although it certainly would function to break the link between marriage and parenthood.

This may be enough to give you a taste of the direction of much of contemporary family-law theory. And in a gradual way, a good deal of it is being enacted into state legal statutes and court decisions even now. These developments raise for marriage and family therapists not only the question of how they might respond to these trends but also how therapeutic theory itself has influenced and possibly encouraged these movements.

Interactions between Therapy and the Law

Some evidence supports that the ethic of relationality we reviewed earlier in this chapter has contributed to the doctrine of private ordering and the possible deinstitutionalization of marriage. If what is really important is the relationship, why do we need the institution? If the relationship is solid between partners and between parent and child, why do we need the formal contract or covenant? And if the relationship is solid, then the kin altruistic ties touted in evolutionary psychology may be secondary if not irrelevant as well. Social work professor Froma Walsh emphasizes relational process as the crucial factor in family health, not its biological or legal institutional status.[36]

In recent years, an entire field of psychology called close relationship theory has emerged and has strongly influenced both the sociology of family and theories of family law.[37] Close relationship theory emphasizes the quality of the relationship rather than its institutional or biological form. The Canadian Law Commission's report *Beyond Conjugality*, which explicitly calls for law and public policy to recognize and support a variety of close relationships and family-like groups beyond legal marriage, is substantially influenced by close relationship theory. ALI's *Principles of the Law of Family Dissolution* at one point explicitly states that legal marriage says little about the "quality" of relationship of a couple living together.[38] And the quality of the relationship seems to be, for the *Principles,* what is really important.

The emerging therapeutic ethic of relationality, in spite of its avoidance of individualism, may be one of many factors influencing these new legal trends. Of course, you will recall that in our survey the ethics of relationality of contemporary family therapists seemed to have a thicker, even conservative, spin to it that went beyond affection and communicative process as such. Remember that the 70.4 percent of family therapists who believed that family form makes a difference for child well-being also held that the "traditional working father and mother at home with children" was the best arrangement for children, followed by the 25 percent who thought the "two-income husband-wife nuclear family" was better than other alternatives. The survey wording of this second alternative about two-income couples had married couples explicitly in mind, and probably most respondents thought the first and most popular option did as well. So there does appear to be an implicit interest in institutional form buried in the ethics of relationality found in a substantial portion of respondents to our national survey of marriage and family therapists. This raises the larger question of public philosophy: should this simultaneous interest in both relationality *and* institutional form found among these therapists gain formality and public articulation?

The New Social-Science
Interest in Institutions

This surprising, if still ambiguous, interest in institutional form among many family therapists does not orchestrate well with trends in family law. But it does fit well with other dominant trends in the social sciences. In the past fifteen years, there have been major developments in the fields of sociology and economics indicating that, from the standpoint of the good of children, married and biologically related parents are, on average, the best for child well-being. Work by Sarah McLanahan,[39] Paul Amato and Alan Booth,[40] the Washington-based research firm called Child Trends,[41] the Center for Law and Social Policy,[42] University of Texas sociologist Norval Glenn,[43] and Rutgers University sociologist David Popenoe[44] all point in that direction.

It is an interesting quirk of history that the law profession has preferred to side with the rather slender strand of close relationship theory and its neglect of institutions rather than the robust data of mainline sociologists and economists. This is probably true because much of law today fancies itself as morally neutral and also holds that the inevitable forces of modernization are simultaneously working to deinstitutionalize marriage and create what Anthony Giddens has called the quest for the "pure relationship"—an interpersonal relationship characterized by a more plastic sexuality and increasingly unencumbered by the burdens of custom, law, or offspring.[45] The dominant family legal theories today are clearly both influenced by an economically and biologically disembodied ethic of relationality and also interested in conforming to the family-disruptive dynamics of modernization, which they judge to be inevitable.

There are, however, legal theorists who are using social-science insights into institutional theory to resist trends toward private ordering. Georgetown University legal scholar Milton Regan uses the social psychology of George Herbert Mead to argue that marriage as a legal institutional status must be retained because of the importance of what intimate relationships contribute to personal identity and mental health as well as for the importance of structured institutions to pattern and mediate these relationships.[46] Regan's argument, however, has little to do with the needs of children and mainly addresses the requirements of adult psychosocial health and identity.

Margaret Brinig:
Law and Institutional Economics

But there are other resources that will help illustrate the kind of dialogue that may need to proceed between law and psychology, including the specialty of marriage and family therapy. The writings of Notre Dame law professor Margaret Brinig help illustrate the importance of institutional theory, both the biological and economic aspects of it. Her work also demonstrates the importance of a phenomenology of the inherited dominant model of marriage that historically has functioned in Western society in both law and religion: the model of marriage as covenant. Finally, her thought suggests ways that the modern disciplines can cooperate to revive a religious humanism that will serve to integrate science and religion into a more compatible relationship to each other without sacrificing their respective integrity.

Brinig is both a legal scholar and an economist. Furthermore, she also is the leading legal scholar today supplementing her theories with empirical research on issues in family law. She is among a select group of family law theorists who address both the front door and the back door of family law, that is, both family formation and marriage as well as family dissolution. This twofold concern also has implications for her understanding of the best love, care, and interests of the child. Brinig's empirical research gives her family law scholarship a rich double language composed of the classical marriage concepts of covenant and one-flesh union and empirical data interpreted by the new institutional economics.

Brinig opposes Fineman's desire to delegalize marriage, Carbone's interest in replacing legal marriage solely with law's support of parenthood, and the *Principles'* concern to make domestic partnerships functionally equivalent to legal marriage.[47] On the other hand, she is realistic about the need to make provisions for the back door of family law—the law of family dissolution. For instance, she affirms when possible the good of keeping natural and legal parents involved with their children after divorce through some system of joint custody.[48]

Brinig preserves in fresh terms the accomplishments of the older Jewish and Christian jurisprudence on marriage and family without, however, becoming narrowly apologetic for these religions as such. She does not directly present theological arguments for her case. On the other hand, her position is theologically sensitive. For example, it is consistent with the integrational model of care found in the classics on marriage and childcare in the writings of Thomas Aquinas, to whom I have often referred in this book.[49] Her position is a kind of legal version of what I have called religious—if not Christian—humanism.

Brinig advances her position by beginning with a step that could have been inspired by the hermeneutic phenomenology of Gadamer and Ricoeur and their concern to anchor understanding by interpreting the classics shaping our effective history. She presents a phenomenology of covenant—a description of the cultural model of marriage that historically has dominated Western thinking in both law and religion. She then secondarily—or "diagnostically," to refer to Ricoeur's concept discussed in chapter 1—makes use of both the new institutional economics and evolutionary psychology in ways analogous to how Aquinas used the psychobiology and institutional theory of Aristotle to shape Roman Catholic marriage theory and much of the later Western legal tradition of marriage.[50] She does this to illustrate how covenant thinking can be translated into secular law's rightful concern with the hard procreative, economic, and health realities of marriage and family in modern societies in addition to their interpersonal relational dimensions, which are the main interest of family and marriage therapy.

Brinig argues that the dominant post-Enlightenment contractual model of marriage that sees it as a freely chosen agreement between husband and wife is inadequate to both our experience of marriage and our past legal understandings of the institution. Marriage, she insists, historically has been viewed as a solemn agreement to a union of "unconditional love and permanence" through which the "parties are bound not only to each other but also to some third party, to God or the community or both."[51] This phenomenological description of the inherited normative understanding of marriage is not presented by Brinig as a confessional religious statement. It is, rather, simply a description of the culturally received meaning of covenant as the inherited dominant model. Brinig then gives a further economic account of its concrete institutional implications.

To understand the social functions of covenant, Brinig turns to what is today commonly called the "new institutional economics."[52] This perspective builds on yet goes beyond the rational-choice view advocated by economist Gary Becker. Marriage, she argues, is more like a firm than it is an individualistically negotiated economic contract. A firm is an association organized to perform a specific function, achieve economies of scale, capitalize on special talents of individual participants, and relate to external parties as a collective unit. A firm is based on a prior agreement—something like a covenant—between the parties involved and the surrounding community about the purpose of the corporate unit. Brinig believes the new institutional economics helps us see things in the firm, and in marriages (especially marriages with children), that the older, individualistic, rational-choice economic model set forth in Becker's *Treatise on the Family* often overlooked. It also helps us see aspects of family formation that the concept of private ordering and its theory of implicit contracts misses as well.

Understanding marriage in analogy to firms enables us to grasp the "channeling," "signaling," and "reputational" aspects of firmlike marriages. The firm model reveals how marriages formed by settled public commitments (covenants) among the couples, potential children, and the wider society develop identifiable social patterns that convey trusted information, dependable access to known goods, and valued reputations both within the marriage and between it and the larger community.[53] Once again, this is a point similar to the one we saw Ricoeur developing in his theory of practices set forth in chapter 2.

Marriages that result in children, however, are more like a particular type of firm that Brinig calls franchises. Franchises offer a developed and predefined array of valuable goods, services, and obligations that individual entrepreneurs consent to and agree to serve. Similarly, a set of imposed responsibilities come from legal marriage with children from both inside attachments and outside social expectations that cannot be easily dissolved even with legal divorce. Brinig contends that the inextricable one-flesh union and the shared family history do not disappear when the marriage ends or the child turns eighteen. Brinig points out something that the ancient "one-flesh" model of marriage profoundly understood but that contemporary scholars such as Martha Fineman miss—that is, that "divorcing couples never completely revert to a pre-marriage state. Nor do children leaving home at maturity free themselves entirely from their parents or siblings."[54] Brinig's twofold phenomenological and institutional-economic analysis of marital covenants leads her to say that "marriage persists to a certain degree in spite of divorce. To the extent that it persists, the family still lives on as what I call the franchise."[55]

Brinig's position is supported by empirical research she did with University of Virginia sociologist Steven Nock. Their findings are based on the University of Michigan Panel Survey of Income Dynamics and its Child Development Supplement.[56] They analyzed the large longitudinal database of these surveys with standard social-science scales measuring child well-being.[57] Keeping children with natural mothers (both married and unmarried) constant, they measured child well-being from the perspective of the variables of income, family structure, legal relation of parents (unique to their study), parental warmth (close to Fineman's nurturance model), and mother's race and age.[58] All of these factors counted positively in some way for child well-being, but—in contrast to the major trend of contemporary family law theory as exhibited by Fineman, Carbone, and the *Principles*—legal marriage and family structure count the most for child well-being.

In contrast to much of contemporary family-law theory, they found evidence demonstrating that the status of parents in legal marriage is a leading positive asset for the well-being of children. Family form is also a plus. Children on average do better on a host of indices when raised by their own two biological parents in legal marriage. As is widely believed in the social sciences and law, income contributes to child well-being, especially in the child's early years. In the long run, however, Brinig's empirical research shows that income is not as important as either legal marital status of parents or family form. Finally, her research shows that Fineman's emphasis on the mother's love or Carbone's and the *Principles'* advocacy of parental and caregiver continuity also count, but not as much as the marital status of parents and family form.[59]

Both covenant theory and institutional economics give Brinig and Nock an explanation for this importance of legal marriage to child well-being. They write that when legally married couples "know they are in a long-term relationship ('until death do us part' or at least until the age of the emancipation), they have incentive to 'specifically invest' in the relationship and in the other party to it." In addition, "legal recognition provides a signal for the provision of all kinds of outside support for the family, whether by government, by extended family, or by other affinity groups." These investments and subsequent benefits "accrue to children as well as adults."[60]

In Brinig's phenomenological and economic analysis of covenant, we have a view of marriage that meets the rationality test of legal theory yet is both influenced by and broadly compatible with the outlines of the integrative view of marriage and parenting found in the Jewish and Christian humanistic traditions and probably in most of the other major religious traditions as well. Hence, her views help bridge the social space between secular law and the dominant models of love and marriage traditionally functioning in American culture. Her work might also serve as a stimulus to a more intelligent conversation between marriage and family therapists and family law theorists. It might help both sides clarify their public philosophies and orchestrate their work to other institutional realities in our society.

I feature the work of Brinig and her associate Steven Nock not to indicate that they are the only figures in contemporary family law moving toward a more adequate understanding of the institution of the family and the best love and interests of children. There are others. But they do merit serious consideration and thoughtful analysis by both family therapists and family-law scholars.[61] Her writings help illustrate the kind of interdisciplinary work I envision that must go into a revived religious humanism.

Epilogue on the Future
of Science and Religion

This book has been written in a range of cognitive modes. As these pages unfolded, my modes moved between religious confession, or what Paul Ricoeur calls "avowal,"[1] to philosophical reflection and critique. The reader will doubtless think philosophical reflection and detachment swamped religious confession and personal passion. If this was your sense of my dominant mode, you are probably right.

But now I want to shift gears. In the following paragraphs, I hope to make confession and avowal dominant over reflection, analysis, and criticism. Basically, I want to share my vision of the possible future of the dialogue between religion and science—my hope for how it will develop and the various ways it might contribute to the revival of a Christian and religious humanism. Of course, this hope has been shaped by my past, by the way I have absorbed the religious and cultural history of the West and the unique ways it was mediated to me by my parents, my liberal midwestern Protestant church life, and my educational experience in liberal colleges and universities.

I have little doubt that this history has formed my confessional beginning points in decisive ways, even with regard to my vision of the future of the interaction between religion and science. But philosophical reflection has influenced me as well, even though it has been nourished by the thick substance of my historically shaped moral and religious intuitions.

My confessional background leads me to value the effective history, to use Ricoeur's phrase, into which I was born and educated. That leads me to envision a future in which religious traditions are still a part of social life in advanced democratic societies. But I also am a creature who can think, critically reflect, and compare. That has brought me to notice times in history when science and religion seemed to interact productively to create what I have called religious humanism.

I hope that this kind of positive interaction can occur in the future. I hope that we can avoid the mistakes of premature speculation, especially of the negative kind found today in the so-called new atheism of Dawkins, Dennett, Hitchens, and Harris. They play fast and loose with the complex histories of religious traditions, and their arguments are not convincing to scholars who know these traditions well. I also hope that we can avoid the closed-mindedness of various fundamentalisms that see science as a threat and that erect barriers and complex patterns of avoidance to minimize its influence on their adherents.

But in order to avoid these extremes and pursue a third path—one that would also lead toward a revived religious humanism—both scientists and religious leaders should consider the path of reflection that I have outlined on the pages of this book. This includes giving phenomenological description a central place in the dialogue between science and religion. This approach is difficult for scientists, but it is also challenging for theologians and religious leaders. Scientists are prone to move too quickly into causal explanation before adequately describing what they are trying to explain. They skip quickly over the meanings associated with religious and spiritual experience and become preoccupied with its finite correlations and causes. And some are tempted to jump too rapidly from explanation to speculation about the truth and value of religious ideas and practices. They shortchange the task of understanding, underestimate the challenge of interpretation, and overlook the complexity of opposing ideas in the intricate history of a religious tradition, especially a literate one.

But theologians and religious thinkers often ignore the phenomenological task as well. They frequently are too preoccupied with defending the faith, taking sides with one strand of interpretation in contrast to another without the benefits of scientific and philosophical mediation, and securing the continuity and survival of particular confessing communities. So both sides of the religion and science conversation—both scientists and believers—need to take the phenomenological beginning point more seriously.

In the future, however, I predict that believers will take the explanations of science more seriously than they have in the past. Scientific explanations provide heightened control and power over life. This is attractive to almost everyone. Even religious fundamentalists want the power that science promises even if they simultaneously reject some of its potential explanations. These explanations should be taken seriously by religious people. They should be reminded, however, that scientific explanations make the most sense when held in tension with the inherited interpretations of our lived experience that make up the meanings of our social and cultural worlds. In the future, we will learn to consult science without allowing it to alienate us from the wisdom and accomplishments of the past.

In the future that I contemplate, we will gradually learn that science, properly used, can help us better understand our inherited traditions. Religions are constantly making assumptions and judgments about what I have called the rhythms of nature—the natural patterns of our instincts, passions, and emotions, and our innate capacities for reason, deliberation, and reflection. And these traditions repeatedly have made assumptions about the regularities of the seasons, the heavens, and the earth. These assumptions informed directly or indirectly higher-level moral, religious, and cosmological judgments, even if the tradition distrusted the influence of nature on the spiritual life. In the future, I envision that participants in the religion-science discussion will understand how scientific views of nature can help refine and mediate between conflicting interpretations within a religious tradition. I tried to illustrate how this can work within Christianity with reference to conflicting views of the atonement and diverse views of Christian love. Countless other teachings would have provided examples as well. Other religions are doubtless rife with similar tensions that science might help mediate, as I pointed out in my discussion of Haidt's criticism of Buddhism and the Christian theology of love. Certainly, there should be no strict rejection of the move from scientific explanation to metaphysical speculation, as happens with abandon in the new atheism. But scientists and theologians inclined to take this leap should understand how precarious it is, especially if the phenomenological moment is ignored or shortchanged.

The religion-science dialogue in the future will help us achieve a more differentiated view of moral judgment. This may be the most significant legacy of the contemporary dialogue. Cosmological speculation about the nature of the universe and the plausibility of the God of theism, which has been a central preoccupation of the past science and religion discussion, will certainly continue to receive attention. But the new dialogue among moral psychology, moral philosophy, and moral theology will be even more central in the years to come. The way in which social and cognitive neuroscience is informing contemporary moral and positive psychology will not go away. In fact, we are still only at the beginning of a major new dialogue between these disciplines that I predict will have significant consequences for our views of virtue and moral deliberation.

I reviewed in these pages the emerging outline of this new conversation about the nature of virtue and morality. It is good to see the development of moral psychologists who also have graduate degrees in moral philosophy. It is good to see philosophers such as Kwame Appiah and Owen Flanagan take seriously the findings of moral psychology and social neuroscience. It is good to see William James, who worked so hard to integrate the scientific psychology and moral philosophy of his day, honored so widely in our time by both psychologists and philosophers. It is my hope that this interaction between moral psychology and the humanities will continue and deepen, making a profound contribution to religious and Christian humanism.

This trend is likely to spread into non-Western religious and philosophical traditions and establish the grounds for a new ecumenical science and religion discussion between the world religions. Science primarily will test and refine inherited views about the premoral goods organized by virtue and morality. Religions primarily will inform the narrative and visional dimensions of virtue and morality; they will help us define the overall purpose of life, its meaning, and its goals. They will do this in the stories they tell about the beginning and end of human existence. Intricate maneuvers will develop to piece together these various overlapping dimensions, something like the five dimensions of practical reason I introduced in chapter 3. Morality gradually will be viewed as more complicated than either philosophers or religionists have envisioned in the past. At the same time, people will learn to become more humble in their moral stances but also more nuanced about what goes into them. In the end, we will make progress in our capacity to deal with the complex ethical and moral issues engendered by modern societies.

In the days ahead, the shape of spirituality in modern societies will continue to affirm inner-worldly values and ends without, I hope, losing the double entendre of spiritual experience and language. In the short run, there will be continued evolution toward a deinstitutionalized form of spirituality. The trend signaled by Robert Fuller's memorable phrase "spiritual but not religious" will continue to be prominent. In the long run, however, I hope that a spirituality located within the classic religious traditions and institutions will receive new appreciation. People will learn to value once again what the religious teachings, ethics, rituals, and sociality of specific traditions can contribute to the reinforcement and deepening of spirituality. Christians, Jews, Muslims, Hindus, Buddhists, and others will continue to value spirituality within these respective religious and institutional contexts, although with less dogmatism and more sensibility about the complexity of religious life and the ease with which it can be distorted. Religious traditions and institutions will be valued within the context of a renewed religious humanism.

In spite of the strong movement toward the institutional disconnection of psychiatry and the mental health disciplines from other disciplines in our society, this may change. The same may be true of the law—especially marriage and family law. This may happen in spite of law's present ambitions to be autonomous, morally neutral, and distanced from the marriage and family traditions that have shaped the Western world. But these recent trends in law may not be long-lasting. They are certainly not inevitable, in spite of the predictions of some sociologists and legal scholars. As we saw in our discussion of both psychiatry and the law, there is new evidence that institutions count—that they make a substantial difference in the guidance and patterning of our social practice, virtue formation, and moral deliberation.

It might seem farfetched to both hope for and predict the revival of institutional life—the institutions of civil society, religious organizations, service clubs, voluntary organizations, and higher degrees of orchestration between professional organizations and other sectors of society. This may seem implausible during a time when individualism seems so rampant. But I write these words at a time when the economies of the world are wracked by poor judgment, inadequate virtue, and neglected institutional regulation and supervision. There are calls for a new era of individual and institutional responsibility. New attention to the institutions of marriage and family has been developing in the United States for the past twenty years and now seems to be spreading to Europe and other parts of the world. New intellectual interest in the institutional philosophy of Confucianism has emerged and was even evident among members of my audience when I first presented the contents of this book at Boston University.

Things change. Trends come and go. I believe a new rebirth of spirituality within religious institutions and a new recasting of these institutions with the spirit of religious and Christian humanism is a real possibility for our time. I believe we can avert the two dark alternatives I have discussed—either that science will vanquish religion *or* that an even more tenacious fundamentalism will dominate the world—and that a new Christian and religious humanism will eventually bring science and religion into a mutually reinforcing relation to each other. This development will strengthen cultural and institutional life in many other respects as well.

Notes

Introduction

1. David Klemm and William Schweiker, *Religion and the Human Future: An Essay on Theological Humanism* (Oxford: Wiley-Blackwell, 2008), 20.

Chapter 1: Science, Religion, and a Revived Religious Humanism

1. Richard Dawkins, *The God Delusion* (Boston: Houghton Mifflin, 2006); Daniel Dennett, *Breaking the God Spell* (New York: Viking, 2006); Sam Harris, *Letter to a Christian Nation* (New York: Knopf, 2006); Christopher Hitchens, *God Is Not Great* (New York: Twelve, 2007).

2. Will Deming, *Paul on Marriage and Celibacy* (Cambridge: Cambridge University Press, 1995); Troels Engbert-Pedersen, *Paul and the Stoics* (Louisville: Westminster John Knox, 2000).

3. Aristotle, *Nicomachean Ethics* (New York: Random House, 1941), bk. 8, ch. 10.

4. *The Interpreter's Bible: Luke and John*, vol. 8 (Nashville: Abingdon, 1952), 465.

5. Peter Brown, *Augustine of Hippo* (Berkeley: University of California Press, 1969), 178.

6. Richard Rubinstein, *Aristotle's Children* (New York: Harcourt, 2003).

7. Edward Scribner Ames, *Religion* (Chicago: Holt, 1929).

8. Frank Richardson, Blaine Fowers, and Charles Guignon, *Re-envisoning Psychology: The Moral Dimensions of Theory and Practice* (San Francisco: Jossey-Bass, 1999); Philip Cushman, *Constructing the Self, Constructing America: A Cultural History of Psychotherapy* (Cambridge, Mass.: Perseus, 1995).

9. Richard Palmer, *Hermeneutics: Interpretation Theory in Schleiermacher, Dilthey, Heidegger, and Gadamer* (Evanston, Ill.: Northwestern University Press, 1969), 31.

10. Ibid., 98–99.

11. Paul Ricoeur, *Husserl: An Analysis of His Phenomenology* (Evanston, Ill.: Northwestern University Press, 1967), 9–11, 87–89, 107–8.

12. The uncovery of William James as a kind of phenomenologist and an early influence on the transcendental phenomenology of Husserl, the existential phenomenology of Maurice Merleau-Ponty and Jean-Paul Sartre, and the hermeneutic pheonomenology of Hans-Georg Gadamer and Paul Ricoeur was revealed in a spate of books written in the 1960s and early 1970s. See Hans Linschoten, *On the Way toward a Phenomenological Psychology* (Pittsburgh: Duquesne University Press, 1968); Robert MacLeod, *William James: Unfinished Business* (Washington, D.C.: American Psychological Association, 1969); Richard Stevens, *James and Husserl: The Foundations of Meaning* (The Hague: Martinus Nuhoff, 1974); John Wild, *The Radical Empiricism of William James* (New York: Anchor, 1970); Bruce Wilshire, *William James and Phenomenology* (Bloomington: Indiana University Press, 1971).

13. Paul Ricoeur, *Freedom and Nature: The Voluntary and Involuntary* (Evanston, Ill.: Northwestern University Press, 1966).

14. Ibid.; Paul Ricoeur, *Fallible Man* (Chicago: Henry Regnery, 1965).

15. Paul Ricoeur, *The Symbolism of Evil* (New York: Harper and Row, 1967).

16. Paul Ricoeur, *Freud and Philosophy* (New Haven: Yale University Press, 1970).

17. George Lakoff and Mark Johnson, *Philosophy in the Flesh: The Embodied Mind and Its Challenge to Western Thought* (New York: Basic Books, 1999).

18. Ricoeur, *The Symbolism of Evil*, 19.

19. Paul Ricoeur, "The Hermeneutics of Symbols and Philosophical Reflection," *International Philosophical Quarterly* 2 (1962): 193.

20. Hans-Georg Gadamer, *Truth and Method* (New York: Crossroad, 1982), 267–74.

21. Ibid., 135–37.

22. Ibid.

23. Ibid., 330–31.

24. Ibid., 189.

25. Paul Ricoeur, *Hermeneutics and the Human Sciences* (Cambridge: Cambridge University Press, 1981), 61.

26. Ibid., 60.

27. Ibid.

28. Richardson, Fowers, and Guignon, *Re-envisioning Psychology*, 7.

29. For the concept of distanciation, see Ricoeur, *Hermeneutics and the Human Sciences,* 64–65; for the closely associated concept of diagnosis, see Ricoeur, *Freedom and Nature,* 12–13, 87–88; and Ricoeur, *Freud and Philosophy,* 436–38.

30. Ricoeur, *Hermeneutics and the Human Sciences*, 90.

31. Ibid*.,* 93.

32. Jonathan Haidt, *The Happiness Hypothesis: Finding Modern Truth in Ancient Wisdom* (New York: Basic Books, 2006).

33. Owen Flanagan, *The Really Hard Problem: Meaning in a Material World* (Cambridge, Mass.: MIT, 2007), 50–52.

34. Ibid., 1–4, 32–36, 163–68.

35. See, for example, the influence of Aristotelian and Thomistic eudaemonism on the modern human rights tradition in Don Browning, "The Meaning of the Family in the Universal Declaration of Human Rights," in *The Family in the New Millennium*, vol. 1, ed. Scott Loveless and Thomas B. Homan (Westport, Conn.: Praeger, 2007), 38–53; Don Browning, "The United Nations Convention on the Rights of the Child: Should It Be Ratified and Why?" *Emory International Law Review* 20, no.1 (Spring 2006): 157–84.

Chapter 2: Broadening Pyschology, Refining Theology

1. Joan D. Koss-Chioino, "Spiritual Transformation and Radical Empathy in Ritual Healing and Therapeutic Relationships," in *Spiritual Transformation and Healing: Anthropological, Theological, Neuroscientific, and Clinical Perspectives*, ed. Joan D. Koss-Chioino and Philip Hefner (Lanham, Md.: Rowman and Littlefield, 2006), 46.

2. Ibid., 55.

3. Ibid., 53.

4. Ibid.

5. Michael Spezio, "Narrative in Holistic Healing: Empathy, Sympathy, and Simulation Theory," in Koss-Chioino and Hefner, eds., *Spiritual Transformation and Healing*, 207–8.

6. Eugene Gendlin, *Experiencing and the Creation of Meaning* (Mankato, Minn.: Free Press of Glencoe, 1962), 255.

7. David Wallin, *Attachment and Psychotherapy* (New York: Guilford, 2007), 3–4.

8. Spezio, "Narrative in Holistic Healing," 214.

9. Ibid., 218.

10. Ibid., 220.

11. Don Browning, *Atonement and Psychotherapy* (Nashville: Westminster John Knox, 1966), 138–48.

12. Heinz Kohut, "Introspection, Empathy, and Psychoanalysis," in *The Search for the Self*, vol. 1, ed. Paul Ornstein (New York: International Universities, 1978), 210; Wallin, *Attachment and Psychotherapy*, 2.

13. Jean Decety, Kalina J. Michalska, and Yuko Akitsuki, "Who caused the pain? An fMRI investigation of empathy and intentionality in children," *Neuropsychologia* 46 (2008): 2607–2614, http://home.uchicago.edu/~decety/publications/Decety_NeuroPsy2008.pdf.

14. Gustav Aulén, *Christus Victor* (New York: Macmillan, 1961).

15. Anselm, *Cur Deus Homo,* in *St. Anselm Basic Writings* (Chicago: Open Court, 1962).

16. Carl Rogers, "A Theory of Therapy, Personality, and Interpersonal Relationships," in *Psychology: A Study of a Science,* vol. 3, ed. Sigmund Koch (New York: McGraw-Hill, 1959), 213–15.

17. Wallin, *Attachment and Psychotherapy,* 4–7.

18. Spezio, "Narrative in Holistic Healing," in Koss-Chioino and Hefner, eds., *Spiritual Formation and Healing,* 210.

19. George Herbert Mead, *Mind, Self, and Society* (Chicago: University of Chicago Press, 1934), 271–72.

20. Carl Rogers, "Theory of Therapy, Personality, and Interpersonal Relationships," in Koch, ed., *Psychology: A Study of a Science,* vol. 3, 199.

21. Ibid., 198, 208–9.

22. Ibid., 208.

23. Ibid., 210.

24. Gendlin, "Experiencing: A Variable in the Process of Therapeutic Change," Counseling Center Discussion Paper 5:1 (Chicago: University of Chicago Counseling Center, 1958), 15.

25. Aulén, *Christus Victor,* 49.

26. Irenaeus, "Against Heresies," in *Writings of the Ante-Nicene Fathers,* I, ed. Alexander Roberts and James Donaldson (Grand Rapids, Mich.: Eerdmans, 1951), 18:2.

27. Ibid., 18:7

28. Irenaeus, *Proof of the Apostolic Preaching,* ed. and trans. Joseph Smith (Westminster, Md.: Newman, 1952), 38.

29. Ibid., 67.

30. Anders Nygren, *Agape and Eros* (Philadelphia: Westminster, 1953).

31. Ibid., 57, 121–22.

32. Ibid., 101.

33. William Hamilton, "The Genetical Evolution of Social Behavior, II," *Journal of Theoretical Biology* 7 (1964): 17–52.

34. Ronald Fisher and Robert Trivers, "Parental Investment and Sexual Selection," in *Sexual Selection and the Descent of Man*, ed. B. Campbell (Chicago: Aldine, 1972), 139.

35. E. O. Wilson, *Sociobiology: The New Synthesis* (Cambridge, Mass.: Harvard University Press, 1975).

36. Richard Dawkins, *The Selfish Gene* (Oxford: Oxford University Press, 1976).

37. John Cacioppo, "Loneliness: Conceptualization," (forthcoming).

38. Ibid., 5.

39. John Cacioppo and J. T. Brandon, "Religious Involvement and Health," *Psychological Inquiry* 13, no. 3 (2002): 204–6.

40. Larry Arnhart, "Thomistic Natural Law as Darwinian Natural Right," in *Natural Law and Modern Moral Philosophy*, ed. Ellen Frenkel, Fred Miller, and Jeffrey Paul (Cambridge: Cambridge University Press, 2001), 1–2.

41. Aquinas, *Summa Theologica,* III, "Supplement" (New York: Benziger, 1948), q. 41.1.

42. Thomas Aquinas, *Summa Contra Gentiles* (London: Burns, Oates, and Washburn, 1928), 3, ii, 115.

43. Aristotle, *Politics*, in *The Basic Works of Aristotle*, ed. Richard McKeon (New York: Random House, 1941), I, i.

44. Plato, *The Republic* (New York: Basic Books, 1968), bk. 5, 461–65.

45. Aristotle, *Politics*, in *Basic Works of Aristotle*, bk. 2, ch. 3.

46. Aquinas, *Summa Contra Gentiles*, 3, ii, 115.

47. Don Browning, "An Ethical Analysis of Erikson's Concept of Generativity," in *The Generative Society: Caring for Future Generations,* ed. Ed de St. Aubin, Dan P. McAdams, and Tae-Chang Kim (Washington, D.C.: American Psychological Association, 2004), 241–56. This essay gives more specifically moral articulation to my earlier book *Generative Man: Society and the Good Man in Philip Rieff, Norman Brown, Erich Fromm and Erik Erikson* (Louisville: Westminster John Knox, 1973; Dell paperback in 1975).

48. Erik Erikson, *Insight and Responsibility* (New York: Norton, 1964), 44, 151–52.

49. See Michael Leffel's extension of Erikson's concept of generative mutuality into virtue theory as taking shape in contemporary moral psychology in "Who Cares? Generativity and the Moral Emotions, Part I, II, and III. Advancing the 'Psychology of Ultimate Concerns,'" *Journal of Psychology and Theology* 36, no. 3 (2008): 161–221.

50. Immanuel Kant, *Foundations of the Metaphysics of Morals* (New York: Bobbs-Merrill, 1959), 49.

51. Stephen Pope, "The Order of Love in Recent Roman Catholic Ethics," *Theological Studies* 52 (1991): 255–88.

52. Nygren, *Agape and Eros,* 734.

53. Ibid., 735.

54. For samples of the ethical argument, see Don Browning and Terry Cooper, *Religious Thought and the Modern Psychologies* (Minneapolis: Fortress Press, 2004), 138–42; Don S. Browning, *A Fundamental Practical Theology: Descriptive and Strategic Proposals* (Minneapolis: Fortress Press, 1991), 158–64; Don S. Browning, *Marriage and Modernization: How Globalization Threatens Marriage and What to Do about It* (Grand Rapids, Mich.: Eerdmans, 2003), 43–49, 53–54; and Don S. Browning, *Christian Ethics and the Moral Psychologies* (Grand Rapids, Mich.: Eerdmans, 2006), 109–16.

55. Louis Janssens, "Norms and Priorities of a Love Ethics," *Louvain Studies* 6 (Spring 1977): 207–38.

56. Gene Outka, *Agape: An Ethical Analysis* (New Haven: Yale University Press, 1972), 9–12.

57. Janssens, "Norms and Priorities of a Love Ethics," 219.

58. Ibid.

59. Ibid., 220.

60. Erik Erikson, *Gandhi's Truth* (New York: Norton, 1969), 436–40.

61. Ibid., 228.

62. Bonnie Miller-McLemore, "Generativity, Self-Sacrifice, and the Ethics of Family Life," in *The Equal-Regard Family and Its Friendly Critics: Don Browning and the Practical Theological Ethics of the Family*, ed. John Witte Jr., M. Christian Green, and Amy Wheeler (Grand Rapids, Mich.: Eerdmans, 2007), 31.

63. Timothy Jackson, "Judge William and Professor Browning: A Kierkegaardian Critique of Equal-Regard Marriage and the Democratic Family," in Witte, Green, and Wheeler, eds., *The Equal-Regard Family*, 143.

64. David Hogue, "Healing of the Self-in-Context: Memory, Plasticity, and Spiritual Practice," in Koss-Chioino and Hefner, eds., *Spiritual Transformation and Healing*, 221.

65. Cacioppo and Brandon, "Religious Involvement and Health," 204–6.

66. Hogue, "Healing of the Self-in-Context," 225.

67. Ibid., 226.

68. Ibid., 228–29.

69. Ibid., 231.

Chapter 3: Change and Critique in Psychology, Therapy, and Spirituality

1. For general discussions of the Frankfurt school, see Thomas McCarthy, *The Critical Theory of Jürgen Habermas* (Cambridge, Mass.: MIT, 1985), 19–22, 40, 272–73; and Stephen K. White, *The Recent Work of Jürgen Habermas* (Cambridge: Cambridge University Press, 1988), 90–91.

2. Owen Flanagan, *Varieties of Moral Personality: Ethics of Psychological Realism* (Cambridge, Mass.: Harvard University Press, 1991), 32–55.

3. Ibid., 29, 336; Jonathan Haidt, *The Happiness Hypothesis* (New York: Basic Books, 2006), 204; Kwame Appiah, *Experiments in Ethics* (Cambridge, Mass.: Harvard University Press, 2008), 14, 121.

4. Appiah, *Experiments in Ethics*, 14.

5. Paul Ricoeur, *Freedom and Nature: The Voluntary and Involuntary* (Evanston, Ill.: Northwestern University Press, 1966), 130–34.

6. Paul Ricoeur, *Freud and Philosophy* (New Haven: Yale University Press, 1970), 494–552.

7. Jean-Pierre Changeux and Paul Ricoeur, *What Makes Us Think? A Neuroscientist and a Philosopher Argue about Ethics, Human Nature, and the Brain* (Princeton: Princeton University Press, 2000).

8. Ricoeur, *Hermeneutics and the Human Sciences* (Cambridge: Cambridge University Press, 1981), 24, 60–64.

9. Christopher Lasch, *The Culture of Narcissism* (New York: Norton, 1978); Philip Rieff, *Psychological Man* (New York: Harper and Row, 1966); Martin Gross, *The Psychological Society* (New York: Random House, 1978); Paul Vitz, *Psychology as Religion: The Cult of Self-Worship* (Grand Rapids, Mich.: Eerdmans, 1977); Frank C. Richardson, Blaine J. Fowers, and Charles B. Guignon, *Re-envisioning Psychology* (San Francisco: Jossey-Bass, 1999).

10. Don Browning and Terry Cooper, *Religious Thought and the Modern Psychologies*, 2nd ed. (Minneapolis: Fortress Press, 2004), 47, 219–20.

11. Ibid., 67–68; Don Browning, *Generative Man: Society and the Good Man in the Writings of Philip Rieff, Norman Brown, Erich Fromm, and Erik Erikson* (New York: Dell, 1975), 53–59.

12. Browning, *Generative Man*, 83–104.

13. Reinhold Niebuhr, *Nature and Destiny of Man,* vol. 2 (New York: Scribner's, 1941–43), 82–84.

14. Philip Rieff, *Freud: The Mind of a Moralist* (Chicago: University of Chicago Press, 1979), 314–20; Rieff, *The Triumph of the Therapeutic* (New York: Harper and Row, 1966), 40.

15. Browning and Cooper, *Religious Thought and the Modern Psychologies,* 67, 141–42.

16. William Frankena, *Ethics* (Englewood Cliffs, N.J.: Prentice Hall, 1973), 14.; Louis Janssens, "Norms and Priorities of a Love Ethics," *Louvain Studies* 6 (Spring 1977): 210.

17. What Ricoeur refers to as his "little ethics," which can hardly be considered little, can be found in chapters 7 to 10 in his *Oneself as Another* (Chicago: University of Chicago Press, 1992).

18. Lawrence Kohlberg, *The Philosophy of Moral Development*, vol. 1 (New York: Harper and Row, 1981), 22.

19. Ibid., 68–69.

20. Ricoeur, *Oneself as Another*, 171.

21. Ricoeur, *Freud and Philosophy*, 291–92; Changeux and Ricoeur, *What Makes Us Think?*, 195–201.

22. Ricoeur, *Oneself as Another*, 176.

23. MacIntyre, *After Virtue* (Notre Dame, Ind.: Notre Dame University Press, 1988), 177.

24. Ibid.

25. Ricoeur, "The Teleological and Deontological Structures of Action: Aristotle and/or Kant?" in *Contemporary French Philosophy*, ed. A. Phillips Griffiths (Cambridge: Cambridge University Press, 1987), 100–103.

26. Hans-Georg Gadamer, *Truth and Method* (New York: Crossroad, 1982), 255.

27. Ricoeur, *Oneself as Another*, 205.

28. Ibid., 207.

29. Immanuel Kant, *Foundations of the Metaphysics of Morals* (Indianapolis: Bobbs-Merrill, 1969), 47.

30. Ricoeur, *Oneself as Another*, 206.

31. Stanley Hauerwas, *A Community of Character* (Notre Dame, Ind.: Notre Dame University Press, 1982); Paul Vitz, "The Use of Stories in Moral Development," *American Psychologist* 45 (1990): 706–20.

32. Ricoeur, *Oneself as Another*, 240.

33. Appiah, *Experiments in Ethics*, 115.

34. Ibid., 117.

35. Ibid., 118.

36. Don Browning, *A Fundamental Practical Theology* (Minneapolis: Fortress Press, 1991), 139–70.

37. Browning and Cooper, *Religious Thought and the Modern Psychologies*, 12–15: Don Browning, Bonnie Miller-McLemore, Pamela Couture, Bernie Lyon, and Robert Franklin, *American Religions and the Family Debate* (Louisville, Ky.: Westminster John Knox, 2000), 235–43.

38. Don Browning, *Christian Ethics and the Moral Psychologies* (Grand Rapids, Mich.: Eerdmans, 2006), 19–32, 193–96.

39. For a review of how this is so, see Browning and Cooper, *Religious Thought and the Modern Psychologies*, 228–29.

40. For a review of Perls, Rogers, and Maslow, see ibid., 62–85.

41. For a review of Heinz Kohut, see ibid., 203–9.

42. E. O. Wilson, *On Human Nature* (Cambridge, Mass: Harvard University Press, 1978).

43. Ibid., 4.

44. Ibid.

45. Ibid., 6.

46. Haidt, *The Happiness Hypothesis*, 67.

47. Ibid., 42, 50–52, 156–66.

48. Ibid., 185.

49. Ibid., 210.

50. Ibid., 21.

51. Ibid., 5–17.

52. Jonathan Haidt, "Moral Psychology and the Misunderstanding of Religion," Edge.org (2007).

53. Ibid.

54. Ibid.

55. Haidt, *The Happiness Hypothesis*, 130–31.

56. Donald Pfaff, *The Neuroscience of Fair Play: Why We (Usually) Follow the Golden Rule* (Washington, D.C.: Dana, 2007), 23.

57. Ibid., 71.

58. Ibid., 5.

59. Ricoeur, "The Teleological and Deontological Structures of Action," 105–6.

60. Appiah, *Experiments in Ethics*, 158.

Chapter 4: Religion, Science, and the New Spirituality

1. For the distinction between inner-worldly and other-worldly spiritualities, see Max Weber, *Sociology of Religion*, ed. Ephraim Fischoff (Boston: Beacon, 1922, 1963), 166–83.

2. Max Weber, *The Protestant Ethic and the Spirit of Capitalism* (New York: Charles Scribner's Sons, 1958), 110–32.

3. For the theme of the impact of the sciences on contemporary sensibilities about the relation of spirituality to the inner-worldly values of eudaemonism, happiness, health, and human flourishing, see the following: Owen Flanagan, *The Really Hard Problem: Meaning in a Material World* (Cambridge, Mass.: MIT, 2007), 1–4, 111–14, 206–12; Jonathan Haidt, *The Happiness Hypothesis* (New York: Basic Books, 2006), 90–94; Chris Peterson and Martin Seligman, *Character Strengths and Virtues* (Washington, D.C.: American Psychological Association and Oxford University Press, 2004), pp. 32–52; John Cacioppo and William Patrick, *Loneliness: Human Nature and the Need for Social Connection* (New York: Norton, 2008), 252–54, 260–63.

4. Claire Wolfteich, *American Catholics through the Twentieth Century: Spirituality, Lay Experience, and Public Life* (New York: Crossroad, 2001), 6.

5. Ibid., 154.

6. Kwame Appiah, *Experiments in Ethics* (Cambridge, Mass.: Harvard University Press, 2008), 39.

7. Ibid., 71; quote by Appiah is taken from Gilbert Harman, "My Virtue Situation" (December 4, 2005), 14, www.princeton.edu/harmon/Papers/Situ.pdf.

8. Robert Fuller, *Spiritual but Not Religious: Understanding Unchurched America* (Oxford: Oxford University Press, 2001).

9. For a critique of the thin measures of spirituality often used in the social sciences, see David Larson, Mansell Pattison, and Dan Blazer, "Systematic Analysis of Research on Religious Variables in Four Major Psychiatric Journals, 1978–1982," *American Journal of Psychiatry* 143 (1986): 329–34.

10. Andrew Newberg, "The Neurobiology of Spiritual Transformation," in *Spiritual Transformation and Healing: Anthropological, Theological, Neuroscientific, and Clinical Perspectives*, ed. Joan D. Koss-Chioino and Philip Hefner (Lanham, Md.: Rowman and Littlefield, 2006), 189–205.

11. For an example of the use of the social sciences to both influence and support the family teachings and ethics of the conservative religious think-tank Focus on the Family and its research arm known as the Family Research Council, see

Bridget Maher, ed., *The Family Portrait: A Compilation of Data, Research and Public Opinion on the Family* (Washington, D.C.: Family Research Council, 2004).

12. Haidt, *The Happiness Hypothesis,* x.

13. For a classic Roman Catholic statement synthesizing Aristotle's view of the end of human life as happiness with the Christian doctrine of salvation, see Thomas Aquinas, *Treatise on Happiness,* trans. John Oesterle (Notre Dame, Ind.: University of Notre Dame Press, 1983), xiii, 31, 189, 190.

14. Haidt, *The Happiness Hypothesis,* 90–94, 219.

15. Ibid*,* 219.

16. Ibid., 220.

17. Ibid., 221.

18. Ibid*.,* 115. See also John Bowlby, *Attachment and Loss,* vol. 1 (New York: Basic Books, 2001); and Mary Ainsworth et al., *Patterns of Attachment: A Psychological Study of the Strange Situation* (Hillsdale, N.J.: Erlbaum, 1978).

19. Cacioppo and Patrick, *Loneliness,* 37, 45, 48, 101, 216.

20. Haidt, *The Happiness Hypothesis*, 133.

21. Ibid*.,* 133.

22. Ibid., 123.

23. Aquinas, *Summa Theologica,* III, "Supplement," q. 41.1.

24. Haidt, *The Happiness Hypothesis,* 35–44.

25. Ibid*.,* 105.

26. Ibid., 130–31.

27. Alan Cole, "Buddhism," in *Sex, Marriage, and Family in the World Religions,* ed. Don Browning, M. Christian Green, and John Witte Jr. (New York: Columbia University Press, 2006), 301.

28. Don Browning and Marcia Bunge, *Children and Childhood in World Religions* (New Brunswick, N.J.: Rutgers University Press, 2009), 417.

29. Kenneth Pargament, "The Meaning of Spiritual Transformation," in Koss-Chioino and Hefner, eds., *Spiritual Transformation and Healing,* 13.

30. Phillip Hefner, "Spiritual Transformation and Healing: An Encounter with the Sacrament," in Koss-Chioino and Hefner, eds., *Spiritual Transformation and Healing,* 120.

31. Ibid., 121.

32. William James, *Varieties of Religious Experience* (New York: Doubleday, 1978), 493–97.

33. Sigmund Freud, *The Future of an Illusion* (New York: Doubleday, 1964), 69; Sigmund Freud, *Group Psychology and the Analysis of the Ego* (New York: Liveright, 1960), 46–53.

34. Carl Jung, *Symbols of Transformation* (Princeton: Princeton University Press, 1956), 55n, 158, 224, 228.

35. D. Jason Slone, ed., *Religion and Cognition: A Reader* (London: Equinox, 2006), 3, 4, 91–92.

36. James, *The Varieties of Religious Experience*, 494–95.

37. Ibid., 37.

38. Carl Rogers, "Theory of Therapy, Personality, and Interpersonal Relationships," in *Psychology: A Study of a Science*, vol. 3, ed. Sigmund Koch (New York: McGraw-Hill, 1959), 208.

39. Ibid., 214.

40. Sigmund Freud, "Recommendations for Physicians on the Psychoanalytic Method of Treatment," in *Collected Papers,* vol. 3, *Therapy and Technique*, ed. Philip Reiff (New York: Collier, 1963), 118.

41. Heinz and Rowena Ansbacher, eds., *The Individual Psychology of Alfred Adler* (New York: Basic Books, 1956), 341.

42. Don Browning, *Atonement and Psychotherapy* (Nashville: Westminster John Knox, 1966), 140–47.

43. David Wallin, *Attachment and Psychotherapy* (New York: Guilford, 2007), 4.

44. Rogers, *Client-Centered Therapy* (New York: Houghton Mifflin, 1951), 20.

45. Thomas Oden, *Kerygma and Counseling* (Philadelphia: Westminster, 1966), 272–82.

46. Browning, *Atonement and Psychotherapy*, 156. For sources on Hartshorne, see Charles Hartshorne, *Man's Vision of God* (Chicago: Willet, Clark, 1941), 317; Hartshorne, "Tillich's Doctrine of God," in *The Theology of Paul Tillich*, ed. Charles W. Kegley and Robert W. Bretall (New York: Macmillan, 1961), 179.

47. Richard H. Schmidt, *God Seeker: Twenty Centuries of Christian Spirituality* (Grand Rapids, Mich.: Eerdmans, 2008), 159.

48. Ignatius Loyola, *The Spiritual Exercises of St. Ignatius Loyola*, trans. Elizabeth Meier Tetlow (Lanham, Md.: University Press of America, 1987).

49. Ibid., par. 169.

50. Ibid., par. 231.

Chapter 5: Mental Health and Spirituality: Their Institutional Embodiments

1. Karl Marx, "The German Ideology," in *The Marx-Engels Reader*, ed. Robert Tucker (New York: Norton, 1978), 150–55; Talcott Parsons and Edward Shils, eds., *Toward a General Theory of Action* (New York: Harper Torchbooks, 1962), 24–27.

2. Talcott Parsons, *Social Structure and Personality* (London: Free Press, 1967), 321–22.

3. Milton Regan, *Family Law and the Pursuit of Intimacy* (New York: New York University Press, 1993), 97–106; Margaret Brinig, *From Contract to Covenant: Beyond the Law and Economics of the Family* (Cambridge, Mass.: Harvard University Press, 2000), 6–8; Eric Posner, *Law and Social Norms* (Cambridge, Mass.: Harvard University Press, 2000), 19–27.

4. Gary Becker, *Treatise on the Family* (Cambridge, Mass.: Harvard University Press, 1991).

5. Ronald Coase, *The Firm, the Market, and the Law* (Chicago: University of Chicago Press, 1988).

6. Brinig, *From Contract to Covenant*, 6.

7. Kwame Appiah, *Experiments in Ethics* (Cambridge, Mass.: Harvard University Press, 2008), 71.

8. Eric Kandel, "A New Intellectual Framework for Psychiatry," *American Journal of Psychiatry* 155 (1998): 457.

9. Jerrold Maxmen, *The New Psychiatry* (New York: William Morrow, 1985).

10. Ibid., 217.

11. Philip Rieff, *The Triumph of the Therapeutic* (New York: Harper and Row, 1966), 117.

12. Erich Fromm, *The Sane Society* (New York: Holt, Rinehart and Winston, 1950); Fromm, *The Crises of Psychoanalysis: Essays on Freud, Marx, and Social Psychology* (New York: Holt, Rinehart and Winston, 1970).

13. Don Browning, *Generative Man: Society and the Good Person in Philip Rieff, Norman Brown, Erich Fromm, and Erik Erikson* (Philadelphia: Westminster, 1973).

14. Heinz Kohut, *The Restoration of the Self* (New York: International Universities, 1977), 132, 206–7, 224–25.

15. For a more extended discussion of this view of Kohut, see Browning and Cooper, *Religious Thought and the Modern Psychologies* (Minneapolis: Fortress Press, 1987, 2004), 223–24.

16. David Larson, Mansell Pattison, and Dan Blazer, "Systematic Analysis of Research on Religious Variables in Four Major Psychiatric Journals, 1978–1982," *American Journal of Psychiatry* 143 (1986): 322-324.

17. Ibid.

18. Robert P. Turner, David Lukoff, Ruth Barnhouse, and Francis G. Lu, "Religious and Spiritual Problems: A Culturally Sensitive Diagnostic Category in the DSM-IV," *Journal of Nervous and Mental Disease* 183 (1995): 435–44.

19. Harold Koenig, Michael McCullough, and David Larson, *Handbook of Religion and Health* (New York: Oxford University Press, 2001).

20. David Larson and Susan Larson, *The Forgotten Factor in Physical and Mental Health: What the Research Shows* (Rockville, Md.: National Institute for Health Care Research, 1995); Dale Matthews and David Larson, *The Faith Factor: An Annotated Bibliography of Clinical Research on Spiritual Subjects* (Rockville, Md.: National Institute for Health Care Research, 1995). For a critique of this literature showing the positive benefits of religion for health, see Richard Sloan, *Blind Faith: The Unholy Alliance of Religion and Medicine* (New York: St. Martin's, 2006).

21. Don Browning, Thomas Jobe, and Ian Evison, eds., *Religious and Ethical Factors in Psychiatric Practice* (Chicago: Nelson-Hall, 1990); Don

Browning and Ian Evison, eds., *Does Psychiatry Need a Public Philosophy?* (Chicago: Nelson-Hall, 1990).

22. William James, *The Varieties of Religious Experience* (New York: Doubleday, 1978), 33–44.

23. Ibid., 31.

24. Richard Stevens, *James and Husserl: The Foundations of Meaning* (The Hague: Martinus-Nijhoff, 1974); Hans Linschoten, *On the Way toward a Phenomenological Psychology* (Pittsburgh: Duquesne University Press, 1968).

25. James, *The Varieties of Religious Experience*, 73–74.

26. William James, *Essays in Radical Empiricism* (Cambridge, Mass.: Harvard University Press, 1976).

27. James, *The Varieties of Religious Experience,* 37.

28. Ibid.

29. Ibid., 39.

30. Dan McAdams, "Generativity in Midlife," in *Handbook of Midlife Development*, ed. Margie E. Lachman (New York: Wiley, 2001), 395–433; John Kotre, *Outliving the Self: Generativity and the Interpretation of Lives* (Baltimore: Johns Hopkins University Press, 1984).

31. Ann Marie Rizzuto, *Birth of the Living God* (Chicago: University of Chicago Press, 1979), 200.

32. Ibid., 208.

33. Paul Ricoeur, *Freud and Philosophy* (New Haven: Yale University Press, 1970), 439–62.

34. Ibid., 463.

35. James Jones, *Contemporary Psychoanalysis and Religion* (New Haven: Yale University Press, 1991).

Chapter 6: Institutional Ethics and Families: Therapy, Law, and Religion

1. Joshua Greene, "The Neural Basis of Cognitive Conflict and Control in Moral Judgment," *Neuron* 44 (October 14, 2004): 389.

2. Lawrence Kohlberg, *The Philosophy of Moral Development*, vol. 1 (New York: Harper and Row, 1981), 191; Jürgen Habermas, *Communication and the Evolution of Society* (Boston: Beacon, 1979), 87–88, 90, 184, 205.

3. For a critique of Kohlberg and Habermas on the relation of premoral and moral goods, see Don Browning, *Christian Ethics and the Moral Psychologies* (Grand Rapids, Mich.: Eerdmans, 2006), 148, 151–52, 164, 173, 182.

4. The two series were Don Browning and Ian Evison, eds., *The Family, Religion, and Culture* (Lexington: Westminster John Knox, 1996–99), and Don Browning, John Wall, David Clairmont, and John Witte, eds., *Religion, Marriage, and Family* (Grand Rapids, Mich.: Eerdmans, 1999).

5. Katherine Anderson, Don Browning, and Brian Boyer, eds., *Marriage: Just a Piece of Paper?* (Grand Rapids, Mich.: Eerdmans, 1992). This was the companion book to a national PBS documentary narrated by Cokie Roberts.

6. Don Browning, Bonnie Miller-McLemore, Pamela Couture, Bernie Lyons, and Robert Franklin, *From Culture Wars to Common Ground* (Louisville: Westminster John Knox, 1997), 201–02.

7. John Wall, Thomas Needham, Don S. Browning, and Susan James, "Ethics of Relationality: The Moral Views of Therapists Engaged in Marital and Family Therapy," *Family Religions* 48, no. 1 (1999): 139–49.

8. Ibid., 139.

9. Ibid.

10. Ibid., 143.

11. Ibid., 141.

12. Ibid.

13. Ibid., 142.

14. Ibid.

15. Ibid., 143.

16. Paul Ricoeur, *Freud and Philosophy* (New Haven: Yale University Press, 1970), 420–30.

17. John Cacioppo and J. T. Brandon, "Religious Involvement and Health," *Psychological Inquiry* 13, no. 3 (2002): 205.

18. Jonathan Haidt, *The Happiness Hypothesis* (New York: Basic Books, 2006), 123.

19. Aquinas, *Summa Theologica,* III, "Supplement," q. 41.1.

20. Harville Hendrix, *Getting the Love You Want: A Guide for Couples* (New York: Henry Holt, 1988), 12, 38; Hendrix, *Keeping the Love You Find: A Guide for Singles* (New York: Simon and Schuster, 1992), 51–62.

21. Mary Ainsworth et al., *Patterns of Attachment: A Psychological Study of the Strange Situation* (Hillsdale, N.J.: Erlbaum, 1978).

22. Martha Ertman, "Private Ordering under the ALI Principles: As Natural as Status," in *Reconceiving the Family: Critique on the American Law Institute's Principles of the Law of Family Dissolution*, ed. Robin Wilson (Cambridge: Cambridge University Press, 2006), 284.

23. Daniel Friedman, *Private Lives: Families, Individuals, and the Law* (Cambridge, Mass.: Harvard University Press, 2004), 9–10.

24. *Principles of the Law of Family Dissolution* (Washington, D.C.: American Law Institute, 2000). This is the authoritative set of proposals adopted and promulgated by the American Law Institute (ALI), a prestigious agency of the law profession dedicated to revising and updating various legal codes in the United States. It is commonly thought that the *Principles'* proposals drift in the direction of private ordering. See Robert Levy, "Custody Law and the ALI's Principles," in *Reconceiving the Family: Critique on the American Law Institute's Principles of the Law of Family Dissolution*, ed. Robin Wilson (Cambridge: Cambridge University Press, 2006), 81.

25. *Beyond Conjugality* (Law Commission of Canada, December 2001).

26. Ertman, "Private Ordering under the ALI Principles," 284.

27. *Principles of the Law of Family Dissolution,* 913.

28. Ibid., 7.

29. Martha Albertson Fineman, *The Neutered Mother and the Sexual Family* (New York: Routledge, 1995), 228–230.

30. Martha Albertson Fineman, *The Autonomy Myth* (New York: New Press, 2004), 47.

31. Fineman, *The Neutered Mother,* 229.

32. June Carbone, *From Partners to Parents* (New York: Columbia University Press, 2000).

33. Ibid., 99.

34. Ibid., 126.

35. Ibid., 129.

36. Froma Walsh, ed., *Conceptualization of Normal Family Process* (New York: Guilford, 1993).

37. John Scanzoni, Karen Polonko, Jay Teachman, and Linda Thompson, *The Sexual Bond: Rethinking Families and Close Relationships* (Newbury Park, Calif.: Sage, 1989). For an analysis of how close relationship theory has influenced recent Canadian family law toward extending marriage-like status to a variety of close relationships, see Dan Cere, *The Future of Family Law: Law and the Marriage Crisis in North America* (New York: Institute for American Values, 2005).

38. *Principles of the Law of Family Dissolution*, 912.

39. Sarah McLanahan and Gary Sandefur, *Growing up with a Single Parent* (Cambridge, Mass: Harvard University Press, 1994), 38, 77.

40. Paul Amato and Alan Booth, *A Generation at Risk: Growing up in an Era of Family Upheaval* (Cambridge, Mass.: Harvard University Press, 1997), 219–220, 239.

41. Kristin Anderson Moore, Susan M. Jekielek, and Carol Emig, "Marriage from a Child's Perspective: How Does Family Structure Affect Children, and What Can Be Done about It?" in *Research Brief, June 2002* (Washington, D.C.: Child Trends), 6.

42. Mary Parke, *Are Married Parents Really Better for Children?* (Washington, D.C.: Center for Law and Social Policy, 2003).

43. Norval Glenn and Thomas Sylvester, "Trends in Scholarly Writing on Family Structure since 1977 in the *Journal of Marriage and Family*" (New York: Institute for American Values, 2007).

44. David Popenoe, *Life without Father: Compelling New Evidence That Fatherhood and Marriage Are Indispensable for the Good of Children and Society* (New York: Free Press, 1996), 5–6, 14, 199–201.

45. Anthony Giddens, *The Pursuit of Intimacy* (Stanford, Calif.: Stanford University Press, 1992), 2–3, 94–96.

46. Regan, *Family Law and the Pursuit of Intimacy* (New York: New York University Press, 1993), 96–100.

47. Margaret Brinig and Steven Nock, "Legal Status and Effects on Children," *Legal Studies Research Paper* no. 07-21 (Notre Dame, Ind.: Notre Dame Law School, 2007).

48. Margaret Brinig, *From Contract to Covenant: Beyond the Law and Economics of the Family* (Cambridge, Mass.: Harvard University Press, 2000), 193–94.

49. Augustine, "The Good of Marriage," in *Treatises on Marriage and Other Subjects* (Washington, D.C.: Catholic University of America, 1955), 9–54; Thomas Aquinas, *Summa Theologica*, III, "Supplement," q. 41–44.

50. John Witte, *Law and Protestantism* (Cambridge: Cambridge University Press, 2002), 210–14, 230–40.

51. Brinig, *From Contract to Covenant*, 6–7.

52. Ibid., 6.

53. Ibid.

54. Ibid., 8–9.

55. Ibid., 9.

56. Ibid., 7. The Panel Study of Income Dynamics has data on a large number of families, ranging from 4,810 in 1968 to 7,000 in 2001. The Child Development Supplement has data on 3,563 children between ages zero and twelve from 2,934 families.

57. Ibid., 10. The scales used were the Behavior Problem Scale and its separate Internal and External Scales, the Pearlin Self-Efficacy Scale, and the Rosenberg Self-Esteem Scale.

58. Ibid., 11.

59. Brinig and Nock, "Legal Status and Effects on Children," 11.

60. Ibid., 6. For other perspectives that are close to Brinig in spirit if not in detail, see Carl Schneider, "Elite Principles: The ALI Proposals and the Politics of Law Reform," in *Reconceiving the Family: Critique on the American Law Institute's Principles of the Law of Family Dissolution*, ed. Robin Wilson (Cambridge: Cambridge University Press, 2006), 489–506; Mary Ann Glendon, *The Transformation of Family Law: State, Law, and Family in the United States and Western Europe* (Chicago: University of Chicago Press, 1989), 306–13.

Epilogue on the Future of Science and Religion

1. Paul Ricoeur, *The Symbolism of Evil* (New York: Harper and Row, 1967), 347, 348, 350.

Index

critique, 5, 6, 24, 54–63, 65–69,
71–73, 75, 77, 79, 83, 122,
129, 130, 149, 162n63, 166n9,
171n20, 172n3, 173n22, 173n24,
176n60
Cur Deus Homo (Anselm), 32
Cushman, Philip, 18, 21, 156n8

D

Darwin, 15
Dawkins, Richard, 13, 42, 150,
155n1, 160n36
Decety, Jean-Pierre, 32, 34, 158n13
Dennett, Daniel, 13, 150, 155n1
deontological test, 66, 74–77, 83
Descartes, 19
Dewey, John, 117
Dilthey, William, 18
distanciation, 18, 22–24, 117,
157n29
double entendre, of spirituality, 6,
95, 96, 98, 101, 106, 153

E

Ellis, Albert, 58, 70, 125
empathy, 4, 28–31, 34–39, 51–53,
59, 72, 78, 99–101, 131, 133,
158n1, 158n5, 158nn12–13
radical empathy, 4, 28–31, 35–38,
51–53, 158n1
Erikson, Erik, 46, 47, 49, 113, 115,
160nn47–48, 161n49, 161n60,

163n11, 170n13
eros. *See* love
Ertman, Martha, 132, 173n22,
174n26
ethics, 1, 3, 5–9, 13, 14, 16, 30, 41,
48, 51–54, 60-68, 70–72, 74, 77,
83–85, 107, 109, 113, 116, 121,
127–33, 135 137, 139–41, 143,
145, 147, 153, 155n3, 161n51,
161nn54–55, 161n57, 161n62,
162nn2–4, 163n7, 163nn16–17,
164n33, 164n38, 165n60, 166n6,
167n11, 170n7, 172n3, 172n7
of marriage counselors, 8, 9, 129
multidimensional ethics, 66, 104
evolutionary psychology, 3, 5, 6, 9,
11, 13, 41, 45, 47, 62, 68, 71, 72,
90, 139, 143
experiencing, 30, 34, 36, 38, 51, 52,
62, 75, 99, 158n6, 159n24

F

Fallible Man (Ricoeur), 19, 156n14
Family Relations, 130
Fineman, Martha, 137–39, 142,
145, 146, 174n29, 174n31,
174n39
Fisher, Ronald, 41, 160n34
Flanagan, Owen, 25, 26, 56, 65, 82,
152, 157n33, 162n2, 166n3
Flowers, Blaine, 18, 129, 156n8,
163n9

Fonagy, Peter, 30

Frankena, William, 5, 59, 67, 128, 163n16

Freedom and Nature (Ricoeur), 19, 57, 156n13, 157n29, 162n5

Freud, Sigmund, 31, 57–59, 62, 87, 97, 100, 110, 112, 113, 118, 123, 124, 156n16, 157n29, 162n6, 163n14, 164n21, 168n33, 168n40, 170n12, 171n33, 173n16

Friedman, Daniel, 136, 173n23

Friedman, Milton, 109

Fromm, Erich, 58, 113, 160n47, 163n11, 170nn12–13

Fuller, Robert, 85, 153, 166n8

Functionalism, 118, 119, 121

G

Gadamer, Hans-Georg, 18, 20, 22–24, 53, 64, 75, 102, 117–19, 143, 156n9, 156n12, 157n20, 164n26

Gandhi, 49

Gandhi's Truth (Erikson), 49, 161n60

Geertz, Clifford, 115

Gendlin, Eugene, 30, 36, 38, 158n6, 159n24

Generative Man (Browning), 58, 160n47, 163nn11–12, 170n13

Giddens, Anthony, 141

Glenn, Norval, 141, 175n43

Golden Rule, 6, 49, 65–67, 69, 72, 76–78, 92, 93, 131, 165n56

good, 1, 5, 6, 8, 14, 29, 34, 40, 43, 44, 50–52, 55, 56, 59–70, 74, 75, 78, 81, 83, 84, 89, 100, 104–6, 109, 112, 120–22, 128, 129, 131, 133, 136, 139, 141, 143, 144, 145, 152, 160, 163, 170, 172, 175
    moral, 5, 59, 60, 74, 172n3
    premoral, 5, 6, 51, 56, 59–62, 64–66, 68–75, 104, 121, 128, 152, 172n3

Green, Joshua, 7, 16, 68, 74, 75, 121, 127, 128, 172n1

Gross, Martin, 58, 163n9

Guignon, Charles, 18, 129, 156n8, 157n28, 163n9

H

Habermas, Jürgen, 128, 172nn2–3

Haidt, Jonathan, 6, 7, 16, 25, 26. 56, 68, 73–76, 82, 86–95, 104, 121, 127, 128, 134, 135, 152, 157n32, 162n3, 165n46, 165n52, 165n55, 166n3, 167n12, 167n14, 167n20, 167n24, 173n18

Hamilton, William, 41, 134, 159n33

happiness, 25, 70, 86, 87, 89, 91, 111, 112, 134, 157n32, 162n3, 165n46, 165n55, 166n3, 167nn12–14, 167n20, 173n18

Happiness Hypothesis, The (Haidt), 25, 87, 157n32, 162n3, 165n46

Harlowe, Harry, 88

Harman, Gil, 84, 166n7

Harris, Sam, 13, 150, 155n1

Hartshorne, Charles, 102, 169n46

Hauerwas, Stanley, 66, 164n31

health, 1, 5–8, 14, 17, 30, 34, 36, 40, 41, 43, 46, 48, 56, 58–60, 65, 70, 82, 85, 87, 89, 91, 94, 96, 105, 107, 108–17, 119–25, 128, 130, 132–34, 142, 143, 153, 160n39, 162n65, 166n3, 169n19, 171n20, 173n17

Hefner, Philip, 28, 96, 97, 158n1, 158n5, 159n18, 162n64, 166n10, 168nn29–30

Hegel, Georg, 67

Heidegger, Martin, 18, 22, 57

Hendrix, Harville, 135, 173n20

Hermeneutics and the Human Sciences (Ricoeur), 23

Hillel, Rabbi, 77–78, 92

Hitchens, Christopher, 13, 150, 155n1

Hobbes, Thomas, 76

Hogue, David, 53, 162n64, 162n66

humanism, 1–3, 7–9, 13–17, 19, 21, 23, 25–27, 47, 54, 83, 85, 86, 95, 99, 101, 102, 107, 109, 110, 114, 116, 122, 125, 132, 133, 142, 143, 147, 149, 150, 152, 153, 154, 155n1

Christian humanism, 1, 2, 8, 9, 15, 25, 47, 101, 132, 133, 143, 152, 154

religious humanism, 2, 3, 7, 9, 13-17, 19, 21, 23, 25–27, 47, 54, 83, 85, 95, 99, 102, 107, 109, 110, 114, 116, 122, 125, 132, 142, 147, 149, 150, 153, 154

humanistic psychology, 59, 62, 68, 70, 73, 113

Hume, David, 75

Husserl, Edmund, 19, 20, 57, 119, 156nn11–12, 171n24

Hyperactive Agency Detective Device (HADD), 98, 118

I

Ignatius of Loyola, 7, 103–5, 169n8,

inclusive fitness, 41–45, 76, 90, 134, 135

institutions, 2, 7–9, 25, 53, 55, 78, 84, 85, 107–12, 114, 115, 120, 123–25, 127, 128, 137, 141, 142, 153, 154

morality of, 112

orchestration of, 107–10, 114, 136–37, 154

relative autonomy of, 131

spirituality and, 103–9

Irenaeus, 37, 159n26, 159n28

Islam, 2, 3, 14–16, 43, 47

caritas, 4, 5, 39–41, 48, 52, 53, 59, 87, 92, 105, 132, 133
  equal regard, 48–52, 133
  eros, 4, 39–41, 43, 44, 48, 52, 53, 87, 92, 113, 132, 159n30, 161n52
Loyola, Ignatius, 7, 103, 169n48
Luther, Martin, 40, 47, 49, 103

M

MacIntyre, Alasdair, 62, 63, 66, 75, 164n23
Maimonides, 15
Malone, Thomas, 31, 100
Marx, Karl, 113, 169n1
Marxism, 55, 107, 113, 169n1, 170n12
Maslow, Abraham, 58, 70, 165n40
Maxmen, Jerrold, 111–13, 170n9
McAdams, Dan, 53, 123, 160n47, 171n30
McCullough, Michael, 115, 170n19
McLanahan, Sarah, 141, 174n39
Mead, George Herbert, 35, 141, 159n19
Menniger, Karl, 31
metaphor, 20, 73, 75, 93, 95, 113, 114, 118
Miller-McLemore, Bonnie, 161n62, 164n37, 172n6
mindfulness, 26, 30, 34, 91, 100, 103

Moore, G.E., 68
Moral Context of Pastoral Care, The (Browning), 58
moral fruitfulness, 98, 120, 121
moral good. *See* good
moral intuitions, 7, 62, 68, 71, 72, 74, 121, 127
morality, 5, 6, 45, 54, 60–72, 74–76, 84, 112, 121, 122, 128, 133, 152, 153
multidimensional ethics. *See* ethics

N

narrative, 5, 7, 20, 30, 31, 53, 56, 58, 61, 63, 64 66, 67, 69, 72, 78, 83, 105, 118, 123, 153, 158n5, 158n8, 159n18
National Association of Social Workers (NASW), 130
Neuroscience of Fair Play, The (Pfaff), 76
new institutional economics, 9, 109, 142–44
New Psychiatry, The (Maxmen), 111, 170n9
Newberg, Andrew, 85, 118, 166n10
Niebuhr, Reinhold, 59, 163n13
Nock, Steven, 9, 145, 146, 147, 175n47, 176n59
Nusbaum, Howard, 17
Nygren, Anders, 40, 41, 44, 47, 59, 159n30, 161n52

R

Really Hard Problem, The (Flanagan), 25–26, 56, 65, 82, 152, 157n33, 162n2, 166n3

Regan, Milton, 109, 141, 142, 169n3, 175n46

Reinvisioning Psychology (Richardson, Flowers, Guignon), 18, 156n8, 157n28, 163n9

relationality, ethics of, 8, 131, 133, 139–41, 172n7

Religion, Culture, and Family Project, 109, 129

Religious Thought and the Modern Psychologies (Browning), 58–59

Republic (Plato), 45

Richardson, Frank, 5, 18, 21, 23, 58, 129, 139, 156n8, 157n28, 163n9

Ricoeur, Paul, 4–6, 8, 17–20, 22–24, 56, 57, 60–64, 66–79, 83, 84, 86, 92, 98, 102, 104, 117–19, 121–25, 128, 133, 143, 145, 149, 156nn11–13, 157nn18–19, 157n25, 157nn29–30, 162nn5–7

Rieff, Philip, 58, 59, 113, 160n47, 163n11, 163n14, 170n11, 170n13

Rizzuto, Ann Marie, 124, 125, 171n31

Rogers, Carl, 29–31, 33–36, 38, 58, 70, 75, 99–101, 123, 159n16, 159n20, 165n40, 168n38, 168n44

Roman Catholicism, 26, 32, 40–42, 48, 59, 81, 82, 90, 103, 135, 161n51, 167n13

Rubinstein, Richard, 15, 155n6

S

Schleiermacher, Friedrich, 18

Schweiker, William, 2, 155n1

science
    as distance, 117
    as objectivity, 22–24

Selfish Gene, The (Dawkins), 42, 160n36

Seligman, Martin, 16, 74, 82, 86, 166n3

Smith, Adam, 70

Sociobiology (Wilson), 42, 160n35

Spezio, Michael, 30, 31, 34, 35, 38, 158n5, 158n8, 159n18

Spiritual but Not Religious (Fuller), 85, 166n8

Spiritual Exercises (Ignatius), 103, 169n48

Spiritual Transformation and Healing (Koss-Chionio and Hefner), 28, 158n1, 158n5, 162n64

spirituality
    inner-worldly, 1, 81, 83, 85–87, 95–97, 103, 104, 153, 165n1, 166n3
    other-worldly, 165n1